A STEP BY STEP GUIDE TO BUILDING A DATA DRIVEN CULTURE USING POWER BI.

By:

Gethyn Ellis of GRE Solutions Limited

(Gethyn Ellis.com)

and

Mark Williams of Wyeden Limited

TABLE OF CONTENTS

INTRODUCTION – DO YOU KNOW-HOW?

If you search for information to help you with any kind of IT change or Business project you'll be met with loads of helpful information, definitions, strategies, tactics, top tips, guides, frameworks, graphs. In other words - a here is WHAT you should do approach.

Put simply, there's lots of great stuff, models, techniques out there. But there is still way too much project failure! (The stats. are out there, see later)

So if there is so much help available, freely, why is there so much failure?

Could it be that,

> Whilst we might understand what to do, **we don't know-how to do it?**

Ask yourself this: Let's say you want to be a Project Manager (or a Sales / Finance / HR Manager or a Data Architect)? **What might you do**?

You might go a course on say Prince II (or Agile / SCRUM) and duly **obtain a certification**. From which, as an example, you then know you need a Project Initiation Document (PID), a Project Plan and Risk Log and so on, and you may even have a decent idea of what should go in these documents, great!

But **does that mean you're now capable** of actually project managing something in the real world?

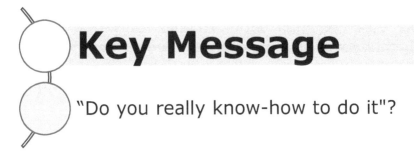

Key Message

"Do you really know-how to do it"?

Key Message 1 - Do you really know-how to do it?

That's our first Key message and it's quite a big question!

Let's start with, why would you know-how. How is it possible?

> Have you had some practical training and advice?
>
> Have you gained any experience?
>
> How often have you done it before?
>
> What really were the actual Outcomes? (Not, just what you put on your CV!)

To use a sporting analogy. You'll probably know that, not all players make for great coaches or managers?

Some do for sure, but just as the transition from **player** to **manager** in a sporting context isn't easy, then similarly surely neither is the transition from **Functional** Director / Manager / Employee; to **Project** Sponsor / Manager / Lead"? Whether that's for Business or Technical roles!

So why do many of us assume that we can simply make that transition, without some training, without gaining some experience. Without some coaching, without a guide?

And what happens when you assume?

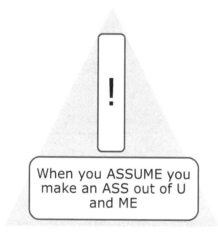

Tips 'n Techniques (TNT) 1 - Do not assume.

So first things first. Survey yourself. Yes, we mean it. Interrogate oneself! There are a few questions above to begin with and there will be more as we continue.

So, go on, **do a self-assessment.**

Just do it! It's not rocket science!

Write down some questions you think are important to you to help you decide if you have the Know-how.

> Have I got any experience?
>
> How relevant is my experience?
>
> Who else am I relying on to deliver successfully?
>
> What's their experience?

Rate yourself:

> 1 is Little or None. 5 is bucket loads!

Gather the data, do some analysis, take a judgement, do I need help, or not? And, just in case you're concerned about the benefit of getting some help, did you know that:

"The ROI for companies that invest in coaching is 7 times the initial investment." (PWC 2011)

And for a little bit of fun, if you asked the new generation of AI tools:

> Provide me with some interesting statistics on how effective coaching benefits employees.

You many find (as we did) that you get an answer like this:

> Coaching has been shown to have many benefits for employees. According to the Institute of Coaching, 80% of people who receive coaching

report increased self-confidence, and over 70% benefit from improved work performance.

Now we did check for the evidence ourselves, and honestly, there's just loads of evidence backing up the above.

So, **do you really know how to do it** because, as the great man said:

"To know thyself is the beginning of wisdom." (Socrates)

We think that many of us do need some help, a guide. That's exactly what we are trying to do herein. Pass on our practical know-how so that you can make use of it.

WHAT IS THIS BOOK ABOUT.

In this book we will discuss how you can build a data culture in your business, your organisation. We will also look at how a technology like Microsoft Power BI could support this business change and drive real value and benefits for your organisation. We will discuss:

- How to start
- Data culture vs. organisational culture
- Challenges to overcome.
- A core framework for change
- Establishing leadership support.
- Strategies for overcoming resistance to change.
- Identifying key data stakeholders.
- Building a data-driven mindset.
- Dealing with resistance to change.
- Implementing data governance.
- Investing in data infrastructure.
- Investing in people.
- How Power BI can help build your data culture

WHO SHOULD READ THIS BOOK.

This book is for business or technology leaders who are looking to use their organisations most strategic asset, their data, to drive value. Some might call this building a data culture. If you're setting out on this journey or if you have tried this before and run into blockers, issues or challenges, this book may well be for you? It's about good practical practice, recognising and overcoming challenges and, acting and getting things done. When writing this book, we had people with the following job titles in mind:

- Chief Data Officers
- Chief Technology Officers
- IT Directors
- Head of Data and Analytics
- Finance Directors
- Data Analysts

Please don't fret if you don't see your job title listed here, as long as you have a need to make your business data driven and want to build an organisation personality that puts data at its core then this book is for you.

Much of this book is focused on delivering business change. We do talk about technology and Microsoft's Power BI technology in particular. Which is a great tool that can help support a data culture in a business. We think it's important to state here you can read and make use of this book even if Power BI is not in your technology toolkit, but it does make for some good examples later in the book.

Finally if you read between the lines, frankly the good practice principles we discuss apply just as well to most if not any type of business change. So if your next project is perhaps customer relationship management (CRM) or a new digital engagement, you can apply what you have used to change your data culture to these too. That's two, three, four for the price of one!

ABOUT THE AUTHORS

Gethyn Ellis

Gethyn is a Microsoft Data Platform MVP (Most Valued Professional), Microsoft Data Platform consultant and trainer. Gethyn runs a small consultancy practice in the UK with clients across the UK, Europe, Middle East and North America.

Gethyn's consultancy practice specialises in Data Architecture, Technology delivery including SQL Server upgrades, migrations to Azure, database security, architecture of highly available data platforms and database performance.

Gethyn has published two other books previously relating to SQL Server, one on SQL Server 2014 new features, and another on the Azure IaaS offering.

He is also a Microsoft Certified Trainer and held that certification for a number of years. He maintains a data platform themed blog on his website www.gethynellis.com

Mark Williams

Mark has been successfully delivering "Business IT Change" outcomes for 35+ years. Over his career he's held Programme delivery, IT Director, Executive and Non-Executive roles in Not for profit, Financial services, Public, Digital process outsourcing and Law sectors. He now runs his own Project coaching and delivery consultancy.

His practice specialises in Advice, Coaching and Delivery to help Sponsors, Programmes, and Project teams achieve success. He offers practical, common sense advice to Doing the right things, right.

Mark posts regularly on LinkedIn about Data, Success, Judgement, Best advice and Helping people.

Over the years we have both seen an awful lot of Change, from small to truly transformational. Our reputations are built on practical, common sense approaches, getting the job done and delivering the outcomes. And that's our focus.

We hope you find something of value herein, that you can easily put into use. If in doubt, be positive! Start somewhere, make a difference.

Working together they help clients with Microsoft Data and Power Platform based solutions, delivery, advice and assurance.

They host the **Putting the Human into Technology Podcast** (The PHIT Podcast), available on most streaming services, YouTube and Gethyn's website

WHY HAVE WE WRITTEN THIS?

We've already said that there is lots of great information, models, techniques that are freely available out there. By all means, google it. Or indeed AI it!

Most of us like to follow a way of doing things, don't we? So why re-invent the wheel? Why indeed! We're not trying to. Nevertheless though, there's still way too much project failure. Bear with us.

A wiser man than us said:

"All Models are flawed although some are useful." (George Box)

So, logically to back one horse is higher risk, however equally backing them all is unlikely to be of value?

In our view, things are never the same from one organisation to another. For a start, one of the most unpredictable influences, us, the people, are clearly different from one place to the next. Even within any organisation it's rare for things to stay the same for all that long, isn't it?

"The only constant in life is change." (Heraclitus)

To be honest we had no idea who said this, so we looked it up, ancient Greek scholar we believe. And we guess today's equivalent adds *"death and taxes"* too. But we're not going there!

So change is constant, and it's likely therefore that the fear of change is also constant? Since time began, most of us have liked our routines. Yet if we don't change, what happens? No growth? No progress?

We do like to use stories to help get the messages across, so here's the first one.

The story of the Mexican fisherman.

Think of it as a parable. We found this version by "Courtney Carver" on "bemorewithless". She uses it as an example to "slow down, re-assess and get real" about living life. These are also good messages for delivering change too. Not sure if it's the original, or why it's a Mexican fisherman or an American banker!

An American investment banker was at the pier of a small coastal Mexican village when a small boat with just one fisherman docked. Inside the small boat were several large yellowfin tuna. The American complimented the Mexican on the quality of his fish and asked how long it took to catch them.

The Mexican replied, "only a little while. The American then asked why didn't he stay out longer and catch more fish? The Mexican said he had enough to support his family's immediate needs. The American then asked, "but what do you do with the rest of your time?"

The Mexican fisherman said, "I sleep late, fish a little, play with my children, take siestas with my wife, Maria, stroll into the village each evening where I sip wine, and play guitar with my amigos. I have a full and busy life."

The American scoffed, "I am a Harvard MBA and could help you. You should spend more time fishing and with the proceeds, buy a bigger boat. With the proceeds from the bigger boat, you could buy several boats, eventually you would have a fleet of fishing boats. Instead of selling your catch to a middleman you would sell directly to the processor, eventually opening your own cannery. You would control the product, processing, and distribution. You would need to leave this small coastal fishing village and move to Mexico City, then LA and eventually New York City, where you will run your expanding enterprise."

The Mexican fisherman asked, "But, how long will this all take?"

To which the American replied, "15 – 20 years."

"But what then?" Asked the Mexican.

The American laughed and said, "That's the best part. When the time is right you would announce an IPO and sell your company stock to the public and become very rich, you would make millions!"

"Millions – then what?"

The American said, "Then you would retire. Move to a small coastal fishing village where you would sleep late, fish a little, play with your kids, take siestas with your wife, stroll to the village in the evenings where you could sip wine and play your guitar with your amigos.

😜 We're not trying to tell you what you should aim for, that's your call. But if it aligns to your purpose, that would probably be a good start! We're also not saying that you should approach selling your big data driven culture idea like the American banker! Let's be honest, he never established a problem, a reason for change. He didn't really ask many questions, didn't really listen to what was being said, and what wasn't being said; didn't explore sufficient angles; he didn't test his premise out. He just assumed! Did he sell his big idea? Doesn't look like it to us!

Here's our first Learning on a Page. If you just want the highlights, it's intended as kind of a summary of what we've said or are about to say, a handy reference point.

LOAP - Learning on a Page 1 - Key Change Considerations.

Delivering solutions to the problems we're all trying to solve start with the fact that things just are not the same from organisation to organisation, department to department, team to team, person to person. So whilst one model might work for one organisation, at one point in time, with one set of people, things are different, and things change! So we have to adapt, constantly!

Paraphrasing (CS Lewis) *"Things are rarely, ever the same twice."*

All is not lost though. Because despite the number of failures, there are plenty of success stories too. What do many of those have in common? Their focus is typically on:

- Doing the right things.
- People who know-how.
- Keeping it simple, straightforward
- Using what works.
- Keeping it practical, do-able.
- Being action oriented.
- If it helps, change it.
- If it isn't broken don't fix it

Now, our book isn't about Waterfall or Agile or Scrum or Kanban or Safe or TOGAF or any of those other great models. They have their place, and we use them too.

It is about those simple, proven, common sense fundamentals that are easy to remember and use, can help most humans, in most situations, in most sectors.

They aren't designed to directly lead to a certification. This is about helping you take actions and get the job done.

Fundamental to getting that job done is understanding that failure reasons are almost always down to us, the people! They are almost never down to the technology. So focus on:

Key Message

People, process, data, technology, in that order

Key Message 2 - People, Process, Data, Technology.

When listening to what we were trying to do within this book, a trusted friend said:

"So you're saying, common sense seems to be, not all that common!" (A trusted friend)

We really liked that and feel that perhaps sort of sums up what we're offering! But you can be the judge of that.

If you take away what works for you, by all means amend it to suit your circumstances, we hope this will help you know-how to:

- Recognise:
  - where you are.
  - who you are.
  - what you can do
  - whether you need help
- Focus on what matters.
- Work out the key questions to ask.
- Check you're on track.
- Spot and mitigate the warning signs.
- Deliver and succeed!

WHAT YOU COULD USE.

You might have a great idea, clear problem to solve, a great team? But you also know that lots of projects fail to meet their outcomes and you don't want to fail and become one of *"those"* stats, do you?

Our approach to help you, is to discuss, guide, encourage, show and prompt self-interrogation!

We'll use fictitious "real world" stories that can be applied in many similar circumstances. We'll provide simple, effective, practical frameworks, tips and techniques, examples and opinion, all to help you dive into your challenges. We'll offer methods to help you work out your specific activities and quotes from those way more famous than us, to help you reflect and understand your situation and do something right sized about it.

Just talking about it, won't get it done! You need to act, but we'll also suggest how you could check and balance your approach, see where things might be going wrong and head them off at the pass.

And if you just want to get some headline summary takeaways, search for our Key Messages, Tips 'n Techniques (TNT) and Learning on a Page (LOAP) and then skip to them, use them as handy reference points.

Key messages

Our key messages are framed like this:

Key Message 3 - Actions speak louder than words.

Hopefully we don't need to explain what we mean by a key message. If there's something we think you should take away, it's this.

Tips 'n techniques (TNT)

You've already seen our first TNT example (When you assume, you make an ass out of you and me). Let's explain what we mean. To us TNT means, Tips 'n Techniques (simple reminders of how to do things), Tiny Noticeable Things (just things that however small they may be, just seem to make a difference) and perhaps even some genuine dynamite TNT! As we've said though, people are different in every organisation and one person's tip might well be TNT for someone else. Or maybe, you see them as warnings signs or red-flag indicators. You decide! We hope one way or another it's of value for you!

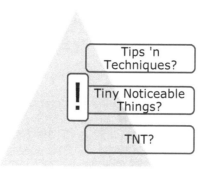

Learning on a page (LOAP)

So what do we mean by learning on a page? If we were running our courses, we'd have slides that contain these points. And we'd then talk about these topics, provide examples or ask delegates to do scenario based exercises to help convey the points. And then we'd summarise to make sure that people have understood. So think of it as the key summary, a handy reference point.

Our learning on a page looks like this:

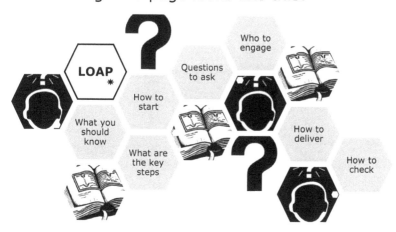

LOAP - Learning on a Page 2 - First things to know.

All of the above adds up to the know-how.

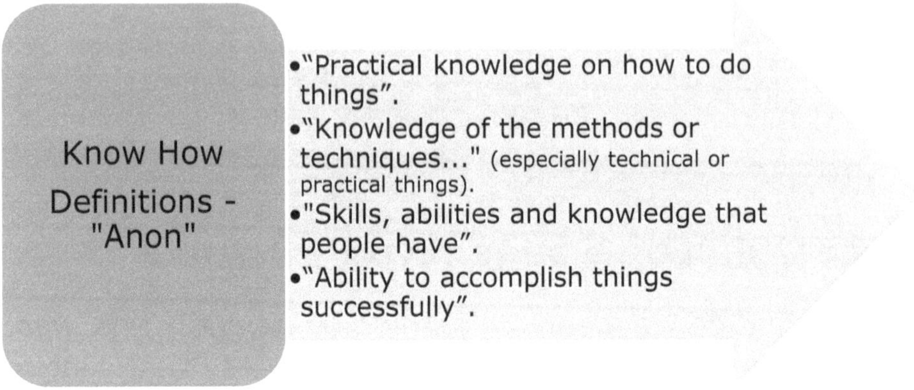

Figure 1 - Know-how definitions.

SCENE SETTING – SCENARIO.

As the newly appointed Chief Data Officer of the Pontypandy Police Force, Berry Wand had a daunting task ahead of her. She was tasked with building a data culture within the police force, something that had never been done before. Despite the challenges ahead, Berry was excited about the opportunity to make a real difference in the way the police force operated.

Deputy Chief Constable Graham (PPF's Chief Operating Officer) had made it clear that he wanted the police force to make better use of data, but Berry knew that not everyone on the senior leadership team shared this vision. Some were sceptical about the benefits of data analytics, while others simply didn't understand it.

Berry knew that she needed to build a strong case for a data-driven approach. She knows some of the challenges she'll face in achieving her goal inevitably include:

1. Resistance to change: One of the biggest challenges Berry would face is resistance to change. Fundamentally, the police force may be set in its ways and may not be willing to embrace a data-driven approach. In other words, its culture was well established and well embedded.

> Write down the challenges YOU might have?
>
> 1.
>
> 2.
>
> 3.
>
> 4.

For example, IT had its way of working and saw themselves as the custodians of data. They could see that there was a lot of work involved, it would potentially change things significantly for them and they saw no reason to change and do things differently.

Other teams such as Finance believe they are the only people that matter when it comes to reporting data and perhaps most importantly, some members of the senior leadership team are "old school police officers". They believe trusting their instincts got them to where they are and see no value in changing now. They could see it was a lot of work. Some members of the senior leadership team may be sceptical of the benefits of data analytics and may be hesitant to invest time and resources into it.

2.   Lack of resources: Another challenge Berry may face is a lack of resources. While she has the COO buy in, she doesn't yet have everyone in the senior leadership team bought in. Building a data-driven culture requires a significant investment in people, training and technology. The police force may not have the budget or resources necessary to fully implement a data-driven approach.

Most people say that they are pretty busy, don't they? That they don't have enough time to do what they have on their to-do list? Organisations similarly don't have the resources, that is money, people and time to do everything they would like to do. Yet, when a new initiative does come along, that has the right support, somehow people often find the time to do it, don't they? In reality, organisations do find the money to do the things they think they **have** to do.

Prioritisation is a topic in its own right and there are many ways to prioritise. We're not going to explore it in depth here, however there are a number of key messages and pointers within that could help you to do so. If you focus on doing the right things, we're confident that this will help.

3. Senior leadership team changes: Berry doesn't know this yet, but about two weeks after taking up her post, her sponsor for the initiative, DCC Graham is going to leave, Graham is currently the main sponsor of the data-culture initiative. This could potentially leave her high and dry when it comes to achieving her objectives.

You can google statistics for average tenure of people in senior roles if you wish. What you'll probably find is that, for example, some CEO's do exhibit longevity, whereas others seem to move on with remarkable frequency!

In our view becoming data driven is not a short term task. It is more like a marathon than a sprint!

Berry must find a way to transcend senior leadership changes if she is to be successful. At the very least, there is a risk that someone she is relying on for support, either moves on, or is focused on something else at a point she would really like their support. Of course she could accept that risk, however perhaps it is better to consider what actions could be taken to mitigate that risk? Or in other words, plan for that risk.

The above challenges are typical of most business change initiatives of course. There will be others that we will discuss as we make our way through this process.

Now whilst our story is about a fictional CDO in a fictional police force, it could just as easily be about many other organisations. At the end of the day, there are often many similarities across organisations of different types. Yes, the terminology, definitions and language used across organisations may differ. However, fundamentally there are customers (organisations, consumers, service users), and usually wider stakeholders, whose needs are being provided for by product, solution and service provision?

Within these, there are people, leaders and employees, who are trying to work together to engage with, and develop their offering to meet their customers' needs. So there will inevitably be functions providing, for example, sales and marketing, service, production, logistics and so on. And they will be helped by other functions such as finance, HR and IT.

Now whilst, just as examples, lawyers, housing organisations and police forces may very well not actually have salespeople, there will be people who are trying to reach out to and engage with customers, who in turn of course may be called clients, tenants and service users.

Or put another way, there are people working with processes, data and technology to provide something of use, of value to their customers or the people they engage with?

And surely the common ground between organisations is that they have, or desire sufficient data, to help them understand, measure, engage upon, improve and even retire their products, solutions and services. So they can work out if and how to improve things like engagement, utilisation, financial, service, effectiveness, efficiency and so on?

In turn this data should provide some insight into the value that they provide to their customers and stakeholders. Which, in a profit oriented organisation should strongly influence the prices they charge, or in a non-profit organisation the costs that they would be incurring. And surely knowing the value (which is not the same thing as price or cost!) of what you do surely is common to all organisations?

Now some people feel they just know what to do, they follow their insight and instincts. And this quote may well therefore resonate with such entrepreneurs, thought leaders and opinion formers:

"Customer expectations? Nonsense. No customer ever asked for the electric light, the pneumatic tire, the VCR, or the CD. All customer expectations are only what you and your competitor have led him to expect. He knows nothing else." (W Edwards Deming)

Now that quote is really about market research, i.e. asking your customer what they want. Would 19th century folk have known to ask for the electric light if Humphry Davy had asked them?

It's not saying that there wasn't any data available to help Davy come up with a solution to meet a need. Let's be honest, *"at the end of the day, it gets dark"* (except perhaps at the north / south poles at certain times of the year)!

Key Message

Data always exists. "No available data", is data!

Key Message 4 - Data always exists!

So there was data available (it does get dark!). And no doubt Davy considered (i.e. analysed) it, and probably formed a judgement along the lines of, if we could see better during the evenings, we could do more, or reduce our risks of bumping into something and hurting ourselves?

So we believe that most of us, even perhaps those above with great instincts, will base their thoughts on some premise or another i.e. some data or another. The electric light probably wasn't invented because customers were asked their opinion. However the decision to invent electric light was a judgement based on some available data and a bright spark called Davy. Probably!

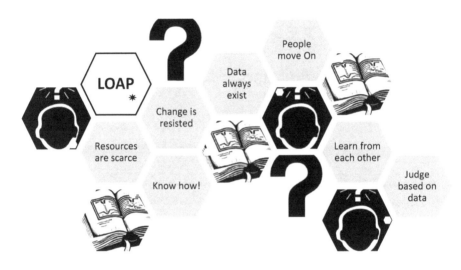

LOAP - Learning on a Page 3 - First things to remember.

BUILDING A DATA DRIVEN CULTURE, WHERE TO START?

What does data culture mean?

Does it mean the same thing in every

organisation? Or even in every department!

Is it about complying with data protection

legislation?

Why should anyone be interested in it?

Who is responsible?

Who is accountable, who **owns** data?

Do they know that?

Who creates / reads / updates and deletes data?

Who might be impacted by changing the data?

Who should be consulted?

How should they be Informed?

How hard might change be?

What are the benefits of it?

When might we get some / all?

What does good look like?

What are we trying to achieve?

These are all great questions, and there are many more.

How do I start?

It's the question we all often ask ourselves before we embark on a new venture. None of us are any different.

We're big fans of Art Williams, *Just Do It!* (See later in this book). But, umm, what is **it** exactly and how do I do **it**? And is it OK if I **just do it**? Should I seek forgiveness, or permission?

Your answer will depend on you, your organisation and, of course, what you think you need to do!

However the bottom line though is that we all need to start somewhere, somehow.

When in need of guidance, we often rely on books to show us the way. But picking up the right book can be tough. How do you know which one has the answers you're looking for?

Or maybe you go on a training course? Well good luck finding one! Or maybe you simply start something, they say you learn more from your mistakes! But do you really want to fail first? Or maybe you just know! Maybe you need a guide.

If you want **step by step, practical know-how** to help you establish or improve Data Culture within your organisation, so that successful change, intended outcomes are delivered, **then this is for you**.

As with most things, there's often several things to think through when considering how to start. Such as,

What am I going to do first, second... ?

Where will I find the time?

How can I get the help I need?

And frankly no two organisations are the same and every organisation changes over time. So what might have worked elsewhere or a while ago may not be right now?

One aspect that's important to knowing how to start, is to know (or work out) your organisation's culture, as getting on the wrong side of that won't help. Your organisation will have a culture. It's likely to not be written down! Organisations often talk about organisational values and for sure these do influence culture. But that's not quite the same as culture, is it?

.

Organisational Culture Definition - "Anon"	•The shared beliefs, behaviours, customs and practices, •that shape behaviour of individuals within an organisation

Figure 2 - Organisational culture definitions.

Just by way of an example (which isn't easy to properly evidence but trust us we're the authors!). There's a well-known UK financial services group that's been around for many decades, who would describe themselves publicly, along the lines of *"we'd value*

33

trust, respect and transparency." We're sure that they do. However (here's the tricky to evidence bit!), if you ask people in the know they'll say something along the lines of *"we're a very risk averse organisation"*. And that is a big part of their culture.

Tips 'n Techniques (TNT) 2 - Culture eats strategy for breakfast.

If you've worked somewhere for a while, you'll likely have a decent idea of your organisations' culture? If you're new, ask around. You'll likely be meeting a number of different people as part of settling in. Why not see what they think needs doing and how responsive the organisation might be to getting on to just doing it?

We all know, don't we, that people often phrase organisational cultural things like **that's the way things are done around here**. From your perspective what **that is giving you is an As Is**. In other words, that is how things currently are.

That's very helpful to know! Why?

Key Message

Data culture aligns to organisational culture

Key Message 5 - Data culture aligns to organisational culture.

At this stage, in trying to establish a data culture it doesn't much matter whether your organisational "As Is" culture is "positive", "negative" or "in between". What it does do is give you an idea of how and where to start, it gives you a starting position. It identifies possible resistance to change, it may even give you some ideas and some priorities. For a data culture strategy to work, it needs to be aligned to the business culture!

But before you "just do it" and align your data strategy with your organisations culture, just step back a bit. How do you know that the current organisational culture isn't part of the problem? If it is, it can be a complex and challenging process to change. However, building a data driven culture could well be a great way of changing your organisations culture, bit by bit!

Don't lose hope, this could well be a great opportunity for you. Before we address dealing with culture later in this book, we're going to take you through some key steps to help you know how and where to start.

It would be helpful to have a view on what your organisation's culture is, at this point. Whatever you end up doing, it's always better to do the right things.

"In any moment of decision, the best thing you can do is the right thing, the next best thing is the wrong thing, and the worst thing you can do is nothing." (Theodore Roosevelt)

Know why.

Whatever **data culture** means to you, it's absolutely vital that you know why you're trying to do it! You simply must get clarity over this.

The bottom line - If you don't understand **why** you're doing something, how can you possibly know where you're aiming to get to?

So, our top key message is:

Key Message

Know why!

Key Message 6 - Know why.

And in our opinion for one of the best reference sources on this, try *Start with Why* by Simon Sinek.

As we said in the introduction, there is lots of great resources out there, and this is definitely one of them.

Don't make the mistake of thinking that you need to know everything to begin with. Clarity does not mean certainty!

You can be clear that you don't know why, yet! Or that you don't know enough, yet! All you need, is to know or believe enough to start, or to find out your why. Even though we're talking about a data initiative here, all we're advocating is that you have just enough data insight to use your judgement to proceed to the next step.

Don't allow paralysis by analysis.

Tips 'n Techniques (TNT) 3 - Clarity does not mean certainty.

What problems am I trying to solve?

The best place to start to understand your why, is to start to understand what the problems are you are trying to solve.

What
problems
am I trying
to solve?

For example:

We are trying to establish / improve / reinforce our data culture so that we can,

mitigate data compliance risks.

reduce the amount of re-work correcting errors.

make our employees daily work less stressful.

focus our operational services on delivering what matters.

make connections with what our customers are showing they are doing in their interaction with us.

> Write Down the Problems YOU might have?
>
> 1.
>
> 2.
>
> 3.
>
> 4.
>
> ...

Start by writing down the problems you think you might have.

And you know what they say: *"If you can't fit it on a single page, don't bother".*

Once you've got an idea of "Why", then CHECK your thinking. A great way of doing that is:

Ask "So what".

Anything you are trying to do, must pass the "So what?" test!

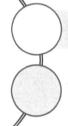 # Key Message

You must pass the "so what?" test!

Key Message 7 - You must pass the so what test.

Example Problem:

> "We are trying to establish / improve / reinforce our data culture so that we can mitigate data compliance risks".

So what are the compliance risks?

> If there was an issue (i.e. something that happened), what would that mean?
> How many stakeholders are impacted?
>
> How are they impacted?
>
> Would they complain, seek redress?
>
> Could you be fined, how much?
>
> How much effort would you have to do to put things right?
>
> Are there external costs involved in that?
>
> How long would it take?
>
> How much might your reputation be impacted?
>
> Could you recover from such an impact? And so on.

If the problems you are discovering and grappling with, aren't worth doing something about, then apply the "*if it isn't broke, don't fix it*" rule of thumb and do something else!

Ideas are rarely in short supply in most organisations. Working out which ones to do and in what order, often is. Which also means you may need some data to help you work that out!

Tips 'n Techniques (TNT) 4 - If it isn't broken don't fix it.

Now regardless of the nature of your organisation, its size or the sector in which it operates, there are typically seven common drivers for change. These are:

Figure 3 - Common drivers for change.

Money: Are you looking to secure new or additional revenue? Seeking to cross sell or up-sell existing services or products? Launching a new product? Or maybe you're simply looking to reduce costs or release time by becoming more efficient?

Strategy: Will investing in this deliver strategic alignment, create competitive advantage or enable you to deliver a new initiative? Or do you need to consider merging or close business lines?

Customers: Are customer numbers flatlining or declining? Do you need to retain and then grow? Are you looking to improve experience? Or are you attracting the wrong customers?

Risk: Risk comes in many forms. Are you looking to reduce organizational risk or over reliance on key people? Do you need to meet statutory and regulatory compliance, comply with new governmental and organizational priorities, or boost the commercial health and wellbeing of your organization.

Your People: Will rolling this out improve the teams' skills base team? If so, so what? Could it help developing your organizational culture? Could it play a role in improving productivity?

Perception: How do your customers, employees and competition view your organization? Will this investment help improve your standing? Or do you need to make this change simply to keep up with the sector?

Technology: Change is inevitable and technology advances quickly. Do you need to enable new ways of working, or more hybrid working? Is your current system approaching end-of-life territory? Is it time to upgrade?

As we said earlier, we're really just trying to remind you of some fundamental principles. **These drivers for change are really just headlines** and they may not be the same words you use, but we've found that generally most organisations think like this one way or another.

You may well have others. Or perhaps you have broken them down into smaller parts. Or combined them.

Many people think of improvements in the form of time or efficiency savings.

For example a reduction in errors removes both the need for re-work (time) and improves customer / employee satisfaction by getting things done right first time.

You may well think that there's overlap between them. It doesn't matter. They are just guiding principles. We're sure you will be able to relate to them though. If you take away what works for you, by all means amend it to suit your circumstances.

Once you have checked your thinking, then go and do a tour of your key stakeholders and ask them what they think. Find out what it means through their eyes. Would changing something cause them an issue or would they benefit from this? Who else do they think might be impacted or interested in this? Have they got other ideas or priorities?

Not only are you building a picture of your stakeholders you are gathering data!

To determine **if you're likely to pass the "so what" test, remember to**:

- Work out the key questions to ask.
- Focus on what matters.
- Do the right things.

 # Key Message

It's better to do the right things, than to do things right!

Key Message 8 - Do the right things.

The right things may well be a mix of strategic, tactical, continual improvement, keeping the lights on and business as usual activities. Portfolio management is yet another big area which we're not attempting to address herein. Other than to say, change fatigue is a real thing, you probably need to focus on getting the right balance over time, unless you really do have a major problem.

Bear in mind. *"It is not necessary to change. Survival is not mandatory."*. (W Edwards Deming)

Is it worth it?

Once you have passed the "So What" test, you should seek to know:

- What is the value to you and your stakeholders in making that change.

Note that **value is not necessarily always monetary**.

For example monetary could be, if we know more about our customers, we think we can increase our revenues / profits by 5%. Non-monetary could be an improvement in customer satisfaction, employee well-being, reduction in carbon footprint, or reduced stock holding or reduced delivery times and so on. Yes of course it's entirely feasible to attribute a monetary value to these as well, but that may not be the way your organisation works or thinks.

We're not advocating that you must make your cases for change to be objective.

If every change in every organisation had to be objective, would anything ever get done?

Figure 4 - Must change only be objective?

Of course the value of an objective change is perhaps arguably easier to understand, but we know that subjective insight can, for many organisations be just as valuable. Frankly, just because someone has shown you a nice spreadsheet indicating revenues will grow by ten million dollars, is that in itself hard (objective) evidence? No! it's just some numbers on a virtual piece of paper. You should seek the evidence source!

Paraphrasing, your organisational culture could be:

"If we look after the pennies, the pounds (£) will follow" or,

"Penny Wise, Pound Foolish" or,

"We Focus on our True North" or,

"Customer always comes first".

We're not trying to tell you what your organisation and therefore your data culture should look like, although there are good principles to bear in mind.

What is important though is that **you MUST understand your own organisation**.

How does it operate?

What culture have I got to contend with?

Who are the change influencers?

When might the timing be right?

All of that is highly likely to help define what that value is and how much it is worth.

Is it do-able?

Key Message

Change, of any sort, IS NOT EASY!

Key Message 9 - Change, of any sort, is not easy.

Change, of any sort, **is not easy** (the project failure stats prove it!)

At this stage, you have an idea of what you want to do, you know enough to believe that it's worth doing, you now need to consider whether you can deliver. **Is it do-able**?

Do not underestimate this question. Most people do! You could add, is it do-able in the timeframes? So, the question you should really ask yourself is:

- Can we do it, without any help?

Our key theme in this book is that it's know-how, not just know-what, that can make the difference. Why do we go on so much about that? Well because **the evidence, the data proves it**!

The Project Management Institute (PMI) often undertake a survey of the profession, (their *Pulse* Survey). A few years ago (2017) they produced some statistics of why projects fail. They were:

- 37% Projects Fail due to lack of clarity in objectives.
- 37% due to communication failure.
- 14% employee resistance.
- 9% funding.

So, 97% of the reasons why projects fail, are NOT down to the product, supplier or technology!

If you search for the top reasons why IT projects fail, you'll probably get something like this:

- Unclear objectives.
- Scope creep.
- Unrealistic expectations.
- Limited resources.
- Poor communication.
- Scheduling delays.
- Lack of transparency.

Generalising a bit (not much, bear with us), there's a huge correlation here. The search list and PMI list are almost identical, aren't they?

Those PMI results are essentially saying that 88% (37+37+14) of the reasons why projects fail **are** down to people! And 9% are down to resources.

Why do projects fail:

Tips 'n Techniques (TNT) 5 - Projects fail because of people.

Tips 'n Techniques (TNT) 6 - Projects fail because of funding.

The PMI's surveys consistently say the same sort of things. Whilst this is difficult to evidence as we don't have access to a time travel version of google, our experience would tell us that, the google list hasn't changed much over the years either.

In the same Pulse survey it stated that 50% of IT projects still fail. We thought we'd better check a more recent view, (thanks google!) and the first article that came up was updated on LinkedIn by Frank Faeth in 2022, having been written several years before (*IT Project Failure Rates: Facts and Reasons*, if you want to search for it). Here's some of the headlines in Frank's paper:

- *According to the Standish Group's Annual CHAOS 2020 report, 66% of technology projects (based on the analysis of 50,000 projects globally) end in partial or total failure.*

- *Research from McKinsey in 2020 found that 17% of large IT projects go so badly, they threaten the very existence of the company!*

- *BCG (2020) estimated that 70% of digital transformation efforts fall short of meeting targets.*

Google may well offer you a different author or article than the one we've used. But we're pretty confident that it will say much the same sort of thing. Tell us if you think there's that much difference. It'll be more data for us, and we'll review and update accordingly.

We're not saying that things aren't getting better over time, they probably are a bit. We are saying, don't get too hung up on the actual stats, it doesn't matter (in our humble opinion) whether the statistics are 100% right or not. Our point is, there's no smoke without fire, so one way or another:

Key Message
Too many projects fail. Often down to people and resources.

Key Message 10 - Too many projects fail. Often down to people and resources.

So the questions to ask yourself are along the lines of,

Are you confident enough that you can do it, or
How much are you willing to risk failure?

without getting some help?

Do you have the
Skills and
Resources to
get this done?

What sorts of roles or expertise might we need to deliver this change?

Here's some examples:

- Project sponsor
- Project management
- Requirement definition
- Change management
- Communications
- Human resources
- Legal
- Data governance
- Finance
- Business analysis
- Process analysis & Re-engineering
- Software solution selection (running an RFP?
- 3rd party supplier management
- Architecture and design
- Integration
- Development
- Testing
- Data analysis - manipulation - transformation
- Report writing
- Data migration

- Support

- Data democratisation

- Continual improvement

The list goes on!

Earlier we said, "*It would though be helpful to have a view on what your organisational culture is, at this point. Because whatever you end up doing, it's always better to do the right things*".

As well as doing the right things we absolutely advocate that whatever approach you take, it should be right sized for you and your organisation.

Fit your approach
to your culture

Tips 'n Techniques (TNT) 7 - Fit your approach to your culture.

In other words, your approach needs to fit with the culture you're working with. What do we mean by that?

Here's an example:

In order to know whether you think something is do-able, you really need to do an assessment of that.

> Can we do this? Maybe? Ok, so what is the basis (or the data / the evidence) of us believing we can?

So, your assessment should be right sized for you and your organisation.

Firstly whilst we think it's always better to write things down, (but even that is a cultural thing) some don't want to. Perhaps they feel that writing it down is too bureaucratic. Well maybe it is, for some. But our view is that this is such an important topic that it should be written down. By all means apply the principle of *"if you can't get it onto a single side of A4, then don't bother"*. Or as the original said:

"If you can't fit it on an envelope, it's rubbish!" (Richard Branson)

Assuming for the moment you think you know what you want to do, you should ask yourself if it's do-able. Ideally you should involve wider stakeholders too, as they may have other input and all that is valuable data to get a balanced view. Here's a simple guide:

EXERCISE: - Write Down YOUR SELF ASESSMENT

1. What know-how (skills / knowledge / ability - see definition) do I need?
2. Have we got the resources (Time, Money, People) we need?
3. Have I / we got time to do my day job AND this extra work?
4. Have we got the support we need? Who's support do we need?
5. Has anyone done anything similar before?
6. What are our gaps? Do they pose a real delivery risk?
7. If I get this wrong what is the consequence for me, my team, my organisation?
8. Are these risks I'm willing to take? How can we mitigate them?

If you are going to combine roles, for example, if you are the project sponsor, who will project manage it? Or if you are the developer, who will test the development?

If you think you can do both, please recognise that combining roles, project sponsorship with project management, or testing your own development, can be a slippery slope.

It can be done, but you need to make sure you are clear about the role required at any point and what controls will be put in place to help you keep yourself to the appropriate purpose. For example. Have different agendas for "Sponsorship" type review meetings to

"Management" ones. Ensure that your developer writes the "test cases / scenarios" before they start development. You should know what success looks like before you start not well after it!

Having done a simple self-assessment, you should also check your assessment. What evidence or checks can you do before deciding if it's do-able and you can do it. For example:

- What have I done before that is transferrable?
- And even if you think you've got most / all of the above,
- How can I assure myself that I am on track, and I will deliver success?

But before you go too much further, you should have a decent idea of how you are going to make that decision once you've gathered your evidence. It is good practice to know your decision criteria before you decide as otherwise you are risking simply fitting your decision to your subjective beliefs, not the evidence.

It is even more imperative in the case of data culture as let's be clear, one way or another, you are trying to do something with data culture aren't you? So you must walk the walk, not just talk the talk! You must review (analyse) your evidence (data) against some benchmark. In this case, that's the decision criteria.

Key Message

Know how to decide before you decide.

Key Message 11 - Know how to decide before you decide.

For example - Decision Criteria - Assessing your know-how:

None	I should do something else, learn from someone else?
Little	Possibly, but I need help, support and time?
Some	OK, maybe I should get some help, start small, low impact?
Good	I can do this. But let's double check, anything I'm missing?
Lots	No Problem, let me at it! Why are we doing this?

Figure 5 - Assessing your know-how 1.

But your organisations culture might require a little more than a few simple questions as above. So just for the purposes of comparing cultures, here's a more sophisticated version:

Assessing... your Know-how...					
"Do I have the Know-how to successfully deliver this *(insert relevant problem statement)* Data Culture Change within my organisation					
Guide - Be as Honest as you can.					
Evaluate your skill / ability / confidence...					
Use / Edit these questions, add your own to reflect your situation.					
Start with the end in mind. First Decide whether you're assessing based on the totals or the most frequently answered replies. Then decide what your "So What" Assessment Outcome means... Would guide examples help you /					
Remember this is assessing your Know-how. It is not (yet) assessing Need, Do-ability,					
If you're answer is None, mark / tick option 1. If your answer is Lots, mark / tick option 5 and so on. Scan for the most frequent replies or add your scores together. .. Compare to your "So What".	None	Little	Some	Good	Lots
Score	1	2	3	4	5
1 Do I have any relevant training or qualifications? (e.g. Change Strategy / Project Leadership...)					
2 Have I got any experience of...					
3 How relevant is my experience? (e.g. Lead, Project Team, Business SME, Purely Technical...)					
4 Do I Know-What I should do?					
5 Have I got any Gaps? (List these separately for assessment)					
6 How often have I done it before?					
7 Have I done this before here? (i.e. data culture in this organisation?)					
8 What is the experience depth of those I am relying on?					
9 How much have they done this before here? (i.e. data culture...)					
10 How Confident overall am I of success?					
...					
Most Frequent Replies					
Totals.					
Assessment Outcomes – predominantly or totals					

Figure 6 - Assessing your know-how 2.

By all means combine the versions, edit / add to them as suits. You know your own organisation far better than we do!

Can we break it down into bite sized pieces?

There's much talk about minimum viable product these days. There's nothing wrong with that if that's language you're comfortable with. For some that language might be a bit technical (some might then get into trying to define what a product is or isn't) and we like to keep it simple.

Having identified what your problems are, can you break them down any smaller? Your solution then only needs to meet that. Once you have things as small as you can, you can then combine into something that makes sense. It meets enough of the **why**, passes the **so what** test, it is **worth it,** and you can **just do it**.

Key Message

Break things down into bite sized pieces.

Key Message 12 Break things down into bite sized pieces.

At the end of the day, change isn't easy. So it makes sense to focus on things as simply and as small as you can. This also allows you to determine what you could leave for another day, another phase. Or what you could defer, if later on in your project, the pressure is building to deliver.

What if I don't know what needs fixing?

Does your organisation have data? It might seem like a flippant question, but do you know whether you have a data "licence"? Well you probably do. Using the UK as an example, the Information Commissioners Office regulates Data Protection. If you don't know and you are interested in data, maybe you should find out?

So, is your organisation a Data Owner, Processer, Controller? (Other regulatory regimes have similar terminology).

What does your licence permit you to do?

Under what basis?

What are you responsible and accountable for?

Are there any special situations that apply?

Do you have a Data Protection officer?

Where do they see their boundaries?

Who else do they engage with about Data?

You could start by interviewing a representative group of **stakeholders** and **build your own RACI based data roles & responsibilities model**.

If you're not familiar with RACI:

Responsible (R)	•Those responsible for completing a task assigned •Responsible to get the job done
Accountable (A)	•Person who owns the outcome •Usually only one person can be accountable
Consulted (C)	• Not directly involved, but input required • May be a stakeholder or subject matter expert
Informed (I)	• People who are kept up to date on progress

Figure 7 - Example RACI guide.

It doesn't have to be formal:

Who might be interested in Customer data?

1. Sales

2. Customer Service

3. Finance

4.

...

Informal questions you might ask:

- Do you handle customer data?

- Do you know where it is stored?

- Do you think we might be holding onto data longer than we should?

- Who would you say is the owner of this data?

- Can anyone access this data?

- Who would you suggest I also speak with?

More formal questions might be:

- Do you process customer data?

- Is there a documented process for handling customer data?

- What safeguards are in place to ensure the process is followed?

- What is the purpose for processing customer data?

- Do they know what the applicable legal basis for processing is?

- What data do they process?

- Does that involve processing of personal data?

- Is any of that data sensitive personal data?

- Would the processing of that personal data constitute large scale processing?

- Where is that data stored?

- Is any data stored externally, e.g. in a cloud, if so where and in which country, jurisdiction?

- Is there any automated decision making involved?

- Or systematic monitoring?

- Do we process data that has been matched or combined?

- How is the data secured?

- Who has access to it?

- Can they create, read, update or delete data?

- Is data archived?

- Can data actually be deleted from the systems?

- What data retention rules are applied?

- Who do they hand off to?

- Are third parties involved?

- Where does the data flow to?

- Do they see themselves as responsible for customer data?

- Do they see themselves as a data owner, a data steward?

- How do we assure ourselves that the data is accurate?

- Where do we store consent? Is there a risk log?

- Is it actively managed and risk mitigation actions carried out?

- What further risks are there that perhaps aren't captured?

- Who would they escalate this to?

These questions are just intended as examples. You should not rely on these in any way. We strongly recommend that you consult with your legal team / data protection officer, team prior to undertaking such investigations.

Now having got this far, you've an idea of your role, and your level of desire to change something? **You need to establish the lie of the land, don't you?**

And perhaps importantly, you'll find out where are the gaps? Inevitably given that you have "data" in your role title, others will expect these gaps to be filled by you?

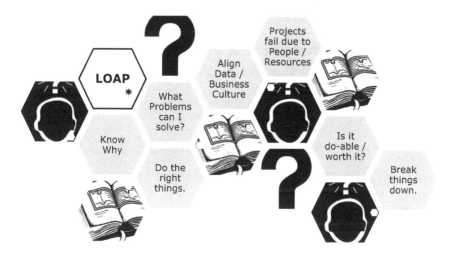

LOAP - Learning on a Page 4 - How to start.

WHAT IS ORGANISATIONAL CULTURE?

You may feel that the theory behind creating a data culture is easy? It may be! But what is organisational culture?

"Organisation culture refers to the shared values, beliefs, behaviours, customs, and practices that shape the behaviour of individuals within an organisation. Organisational culture is the collective personality of the organisation and how it influences how people interact with each other, how decisions are made, and how work is done." (Our summary of various sources such as, Ravasi and Schultz, Dean and Kennedy, Kotter)

In our experience, organisational culture is often referred to as the way things are done around here. It's often unstated and difficult to explain. It's the unseen influencing hand on the tiller. It's the feel. It just IS!

Has anyone ever told you, "*That's not how we do things around here*"? We bet they have! Maybe not in those exact words.

So given that culture is inherently linked with people, and change isn't easy, and people are one of the biggest reasons why projects fail or succeed, our view is that it is the practical implementation that can prove challenging.

Various factors, including the history and values of the organisation, the leadership style, the nature of the work, and the external environment, amongst other things can influence organisational culture.

A strong positive organisational culture can lead to a more engaged and committed workforce, improved productivity, and better outcomes for the business. On the other hand, a negative, harmful or toxic culture can lead to high turnover, low morale, and poor performance.

There are many, many great textbooks on organisational culture out there. This book is not intended to about organisational change, but building a data culture will likely require some change in the organisational culture at some level. Organisational culture is both top down **AND** bottom up.

Therefore, organisational culture can have a real influence on the business.

Key Message

Culture is both top down and bottom up.

Key Message 13 Culture is top down and bottom up.

Data culture means cultural change.

Building a data culture may mean changing the culture of the organisation or business. It will of course depend on your starting point. So knowing whether your objective is to establish, improve or reinforce is key.

Changing culture might sound like a big thing to change, and in all likelihood, it probably is a big change. It can be a complex and challenging process. It definitely will take time and persistence, but it is possible with the right approach and commitment from senior leadership.

If you're not clear how much of an impact your organisational culture is likely to have on the success or failure of your data driven culture change, at the very least - you're failing to plan, and probably planning to fail!

Failing to Plan, is planning to Fail!

Tips 'n Techniques (TNT) 8 - Failing to plan, is planning to fail.

If you've worked within your organisation for some time AND have been involved with, or even led other changes, you probably have an idea of "how things are done around here?"

If you're new, (like Berry) then maybe you haven't yet experienced much of it yourself? Or aren't as yet sure?

Our point though is, that in the same way for example that you need to know your why, you also need to understand the culture, therefore the **environment** that you're dealing with.

YOU NEED TO KNOW how much influence your organisations culture impacts your success!

Changing organisational culture

We trust that you can see organisational culture is linked to the success of building a data culture. Every organisation has its culture. We don't want this book to trivialise changing organisational culture, it is not easy!

Does that mean you shouldn't start? Or that you have to address culture first?

You should definitely start.

But quite often in order to get people to buy-in to any greater vision, it is helpful to have some **pilots which prove that change can bring benefits**. In other words, some evidence, some data.

Frankly any significant change, including organisation culture change, doesn't happen overnight. It is often a combination of smaller actions that subtly bring lasting positive change.

So perhaps data could be an example of such a pilot within your organisation?

These high-level steps are listed here, and each step might need lots of concerted effort over a sustained period. Changing organisational culture is not quick, but the high-level steps that can bring organisational change are listed here. For example, if you change your business culture to a data culture, the business can use their data better.

The high-level steps depicted below can help change an organisation's culture, large and small.

- Assess the current culture: Conduct an assessment to understand the key values, beliefs, and behaviours that shape the organisation. This can be done through surveys, focus groups, and observing behaviours and practices.

- Identify the desired culture: Identify the desired culture that the organisation wants to achieve. This can be done by defining the organisation's values, vision, and mission statement. (This may well be hard to do and agree upon. Others may feel that this isn't your area! Don't step on other's shoes! Start small, perhaps fix your own world first?)

- Develop a plan: Develop a plan to change the culture, including specific actions and initiatives that will help shift behaviours and practices in the desired direction.

- Involve employees: Involve employees in the change process by seeking their input, engaging them in discussions about the desired culture, and encouraging their participation in culture change initiatives.

- Lead by example: Leaders must lead by example and model the desired behaviours and practices. This can involve changing leadership styles, communication methods, and decision-making processes.

- Training and resources: To help employees develop the skills and knowledge needed to operate in the desired culture. This can include training on new technologies, communication skills, and conflict resolution.

- Monitor progress towards the desired culture and adjust the plan as needed.

- Celebrate successes and recognise employees' efforts to contribute to the change process.

Figure 8 - Steps involved in changing data culture.

Remember we said at the start that successful project practices include:

- Keep it simple.

- Use proven techniques.

- Keep it practical.

- Be action oriented.

- Just do It!

Whilst this book is about data culture, the above is good, time proven practice for all projects! It's not rocket science. It is common sense. Sadly common sense isn't always as common as one might think! However many successful change initiatives do follow something very close to the above. Don't re-create the wheel. You don't need to. The above works. **Just do it!**

Now let us just pause for a moment and reflect on the above key steps. And as any good tradesman will tell you:

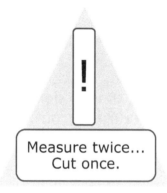

Tips 'n Techniques (TNT) 9 - Measure twice, cut once.

So, what are we really saying?

- Do an "As is". Find out how things really are, what problems and ideas exist? Who might support a data initiative, who you might need to work on. How can you know what you need to change if you don't know your start point?

- Do a "To be". Consider different ways you can get there. Start with the end in mind. Don't over commit. How can you know your "To be" if you don't know your why?

- Plan! Plan your work, work your plan. Check plans with stakeholders, start the buy-in process. Listen. Consider the feedback. Amend your thinking.

- Evidence your progress (examples, pilots, proof of concept, walk the walk). How can you change data culture if you don't share the data, the progress, and solutions you're delivering?

- Help people change. How will people change if you don't encourage them, show them how, provide resources?

- Review your outcomes, make further incremental change. How will you embed data cultural change if you'd don't review your data outcomes and change based further based on what the data is saying!

One of our top principles to just get on and do any or all of the above steps is our take on another great one from Professor Deming. Plan - Do - Check - Act. In this context we've used it to help assess organisational culture. But it's a great general technique.

Someone we know once called the plan - do - check - act model, **the ultimate success formula**!

Perhaps because it is so versatile and really easy to remember. You can apply it to pretty much any change you're thinking of doing.

In the context of data it is walking the walk! You're thinking (plan), gathering some data (do), analysing (check) and being data driven (act)? Our version adds in clarity to help you check your facts, your evidence, your data as you go along.

Plan - Do - Check - Act.

So you start by wanting to assess the current culture. How do you do that?

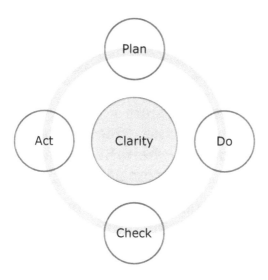

Figure 9 - Plan - Do - Check - Act.

You plan it.

For example. What do I need to know to assess data culture? You write a list. Perhaps some of that list is factual.

> What is data?
> Where is it found?
> Who owns data?
> What data do you work with?

Perhaps some of it is multiple choice? From the following [insert consideration], what are the top 3 issues that cause negative customer feedback or complaints?

Perhaps some of what you're trying to gather is ideas? e.g. what problems do we have? Do we have data culture issues, what are they?

OK, these questions are simplistic, they are intended to make you think, start the process, find out what is likely to work for you.

Then you do it.

But perhaps you should start small, in your own areas first. **Even if you're the Chief Data Officer you would still probably benefit from trialling** i.e. piloting or testing your approach somewhere first?

Now your organisational culture may well influence whether the best place to test your approach is in the toughest nut to crack or amongst friends. Or maybe a bit of both. That's your call.

Your pilot "do it" though, could be as simple as a workshop with your own team. What's a couple of hours effort to gather some data, check thinking, test a method?

Then you check it.

> What are the answers to the questions we've asked?

> What direction of travel are they suggesting?

What do we need to change? Our,

Questions

Approach

Method

Engagement etc.

Are we confident that we can rely on this data?

Is it right?

What actual, factual evidence do we have?

Then you act on that.

Which might mean you revise your questions etc. and do it again. Or it might (hopefully) mean that you can go onto your next stage (perhaps engaging a wider test audience) albeit with some improved questions or method.

And remember to take people with you on your data cultural journey. You absolutely should tell them, what has happened already, what you have changed and hence why you are now doing it this way. It's all data!

Once you have sufficiently assessed your current culture, you can move onto trying to work out what the future should be, your target, desired data culture. Now of course, whether you have a formal check point before moving from stage 1 (assess current culture) to step 2 (identify desired culture) is down to you. Your organisation may work that way ("*You can't pass Go until you've collected £/$ 400*", e.g. a formal check, you have to seek permission before proceeding, is the culture) or equally it may be a bit more fluid (some may say agile) and work on the solutions alongside firming up all the starting points and the problems. Which of course may be influenced by the resources you have to deploy for this.

Just remember: When you assume you make an ass out you and me. Consider **timing is everything!** So test the water first.

Tips 'n Techniques (TNT) 10 - When you assume, you make an ass out of you and me.

Tips 'n Techniques (TNT) 11 - Timing is everything.

WHAT IS A CHIEF DATA OFFICER (CDO)

A Chief Data Officer (CDO) is an executive-level position in an organisation responsible for managing, protecting, and leveraging the organisation's data assets. The CDO is typically responsible for developing and implementing data strategy, ensuring data quality, overseeing data governance, and ensuring compliance with data privacy regulations. The CDO may also be responsible for identifying and implementing new technologies and tools to support data management and analysis and leading efforts to integrate data from disparate sources and analyse it to derive insights and drive decision-making. The CDO may work closely with other executives, such as the Chief Information Officer (CIO) and Chief Technology Officer (CTO), and with business leaders throughout the organisation.

We're giving you this definition here as the leading character in our story is Berry Wand, who has just secured her first Chief Data Officer role with Pontypandy Police Force.

Berry Wand is our Chief Data Officer

We like to turn content into a bit of a story, with characters experiencing real-life problems that you might be experiencing too and can resonate with the issues facing our characters. All characters and organisations used in our content are fictional. So, with that said, let's re-introduce you to Berry Wand.

Berry Wand was feeling upbeat. She had just secured her first Chief Data Officer Role for a police force in Wales in the UK. We'll pinch the fictional region of PontyPandy from Gethyn's son's favourite cartoon on TV, Fireman Sam. Berry works for PontyPandy Police Force (PPF)

As the Chief Data Officer for a leading police force, she was in charge of creating a data-driven corporate culture. She thinks she probably has enough tools she needs to make it happen. But she needed to figure out where to start; she had a vision, but felt it was the implementation and delivery of that vision that she needed help with.

Are you a data officer?

We said at the outset that this book is for business or technology leaders who are looking to use their organisations most strategic asset, their data, to drive value. Whilst there are more and more organisations who are employing Chief Data Officers, for many though **data is often a subpart of someone's role**.

If you asked users who was responsible for data, they would probably mention IT and Finance without thinking too hard about it, but it could easily be people dealing with customer relationship management, operational data, websites, employees and so on.

Wherever you sit within your organisation, if data is a part of or your full role, and you think change relating to data is needed, here's a great quote from Barack Obama to bear in mind.

"Change will not come if we wait for some other person or some other time. We are the ones we've been waiting for. We are the change that we seek." (Barack Obama)

Or to edit Art Williams, "*Just get on and do it!*"

SPECIFIC DATA CULTURE CHALLENGES FACING CDOs.

We have established that if you have to build a data culture, as opposed to refresh it for example, it is highly likely to co-exist with changing organisational culture. Bringing this back to Berry and her CDO role at Pontypandy Police. She has encountered some specific issues when changing organisational behaviour to be more data driven.

Deputy Chief Constable Graham had made it clear that he wanted the police force to make better use of data, but Berry knew that not everyone on the senior leadership team shared this vision. Some were sceptical about the benefits of data analytics, while others simply didn't understand it.

Here are some key examples of the challenges typically faced in building, improving and possibly in refreshing data culture. Berry knows she is facing some of these and perhaps most of them.

But it's still early on in her tenure, she doesn't know, what she doesn't know!

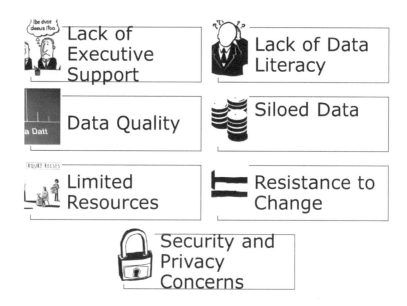

Figure 10 - Specific data culture challenges facing CDO's.

- Lack of executive support: Building a data culture requires strong executive support, and CDOs may need it to get the resources and buy-in they need to succeed.

  Recently, DCC Graham, the Chief Operating Officer who brought her in, her executive sponsor at the board level, left. We'll leave the argument that a CDO should be at the board level for another day. Berry was in a situation where her executive support at the highest level of the organisation had left. Some other senior leadership team members liked the idea but were less invested than the old COO.

- Resistance to change. Building a data culture can mean introducing change. People do resist change, sometimes obviously, sometimes not so.

  Sometimes that change can lead to responses like, "That's not how we do things around here". Berry has encountered this from several stakeholders. There are plenty of "old school" officers who have done things their own way, and even if they were open to change, changing years of habits and practices just isn't easy. But at least those that say "we don't do it that way" have actually said so. Berry does at least know there is a challenge to overcome. Some stakeholders / users simply ignore the change and Berry will be none the wiser for weeks to come.

  Changing organisational culture, change in general can be a complex and slow process, and some employees may be resistant to change or unwilling to adopt new technologies or practices. Berry will need to overcome some of this resistance if she will have any chance of success.

- Siloed data: In many organisations, data is siloed and difficult to access or analyse. Different applications have different data stores on different technology. E.g.:

  New digital solutions not properly integrated into legacy back office systems, as it's difficult and takes a long time to get right. Similarly operational ordering, storing and supply solutions often simply "journal" information across into

Finance systems (i.e. summary data), as richer data whilst preferable, might risk financial statements. Employee utilisation information (e.g. timesheets at is simplest) usually isn't linked to HR. Customer / Service user engagement is built on home grown applications (e.g. survey type) requiring lots of re-keying. Effectiveness / Efficiency can't really be measured as there is no holistic view.

Furthermore, Data comes in different types, shapes and sizes. E.g. Structured data is found in applications, i.e. data entry fields. But unstructured data also exists in these applications (e.g. free text fields) and also commonly in other, often communication based applications, such as email, chat, messaging and so on. Both types of data can contain valuable insight! And then there's the plethora of general data stores, e.g. File shares / folders; Document Management systems (e.g. SharePoint), OneNote type systems where all sorts of stuff are lodged. Longer term employees are used to this, it's just how it is. Much of their day is spent looking for where they know the right data is stored, checking multiple stores so they are confident they have the full picture or just re-keying to try and keep things in line. And on top of that even if they fully recognise how frustrating all that is, if that isn't needed anymore, they might be worried for their future?

Finally, suppose there is no data warehouse or master data? In that case, it can be difficult for CDOs to build a unified view of the organisation's data or develop insights to inform decision-making. But even if there were, just because there is data in a data warehouse, doesn't mean that the data is right!

- Data quality issues: Data quality issues, such as incomplete or inaccurate data, can undermine the credibility of data-driven decision-making and make building trust in the data challenging.

There are many influences on data quality. Not just the obvious of whether you spell it as Davies or Davis. For example, very often there is little understanding, of what system should be / is the master system of record for that data type. Put another way, which system is your organisation truly relying on for the correct details of their customer / contact / service user? Is that the CRM Solution? The Finance system? Or say an employee's details. Inevitably their details will be in HR, but they will also be in an IT helpdesk / service system too? Which one is to be trusted? For sure salaries are in the HR world, but what if someone gets married, changes their name? Maybe that should be the IT system as that's what controls usernames and passwords; Maybe not.

Data quality issues can be caused by lack of attention to detail, training or simply ignorance of what changing certain data might actually mean for other users. That said poor controls and governance are also just as likely to impact.

What you can be confident about is the old adage:

Garbage in...
Garbage Out

Tips 'n Techniques (TNT) 12 - Garbage in, garbage out.

- Lack of data literacy: Building a data culture requires that employees have a basic level of data literacy, but many employees may need more skills or knowledge to analyse and interpret data effectively.

- Gartner says the definition of data literacy is:

And, from their 2017 Annual Chief Data Officer Survey, Gartner say that *"Data Literacy is the 2nd biggest internal roadblock to success of CDO's!"*

Data Literacy
Definition -
Gartner

The Ability to...

- Read, write & communicate data in context
- Understand data sources, contructs, analytical methods and techniques.
- Describe the use case, application and resulting value
- Use existing / emerging techology to deliver better business outcomes

Figure 11 - Definition of Data Literacy.

And, to repeat... from their 2017 Annual Chief Data Officer Survey, Gartner say that *"Data Literacy is the 2nd biggest internal roadblock to success of CDO's!"*

To simplify this, if you / your users don't understand it (data), don't know how to engage others on the subject, can't describe the value / outcomes you might get from it, you're not in a great place!

Ask yourself this: How many of us are really, truly "excellent" on Word, PowerPoint, Excel? Yes of course some are. But we think there's some truth in the thought that users probably only know what they know, and then probably forget things if they don't use it often enough?

And given that software continues to change pretty fast, if you apply all that thinking to Data, what is the likelihood that your users are data literate? (Whatever definition works for you). And if they are, how much re-enforcement needs to be done?

So, **maybe one of your first tasks should be to improve data literacy** before you even start to introduce new tools and techniques?

OK, but that (a) might not grab people's attention and (b) might well take a while. However:

Key Message

You can't build on shifting sand!

Key Message 14 - You can't build on shifting sand.

So, one way or another you're likely to need to tackle data literacy, but, be prepared for the longer game!

Oh and by the way, the top roadblock that Gartner suggested in the same survey was, "culture"! *(To repeat -"top... culture"!)*

- Security and privacy concerns: Data security and privacy are important when working with data,

CDOs must ensure appropriate safeguards are in place to protect sensitive data. E.g.

GDPR came into force in the EU on the 25th of May 2018. Lots of countries have similar. By similar we simply mean that inevitably wherever in the world you are or trade in, there will be legislation and guidance you should be aware of. (This book isn't about legislation). On top of that, Cyber security, to protect your data as well as your systems, networks and so on, is one of the top topics keeping IT leaders up at night. And as technology continues to change, this concern is here to stay surely?

Bottom line, as a CDO (or similar), **do you really know where all your data is, who has / shouldn't have access? What levels of protection should or shouldn't be in place? What are you relying on as your source of the truth**? This, in our humble opinion, isn't something you should be assuming or guessing at. You need to know! Maybe this is your starting point? What data risks are your responsibility or others think are your responsibility?

- Limited resources: Building a data culture requires significant technology, training, and data governance investments. CDOs may need help to secure the resources they need to build a robust data culture. For this, we've not offered examples, just simply a question.

o *"What organisation has sufficient resources to do everything it wants to do?"*

So there are lot of data challenges; you may well have more. And you're going to have to compete with lots of other well intended initiatives too.

And if this wasn't enough, in Berry's case, her organisation is also part of a much wider community with systems and data being made available from the "centralised community" i.e. national systems.

As things stand, she has no influence over these whatsoever, yet her users are required to use such systems. And if these systems / initiatives have similar challenges to the above, what do you do when you know the data is wrong? Or, at least through your eyes, it looks wrong! Maybe the data is right and you're not?

Are you part of a larger group? Or do you benchmark data with others in your sector, for overall sector improvement? Maybe you have similar considerations?

A STEP BY STEP GUIDE TO BUILDING A DATA CULTURE.

Building, reenergising, improving or refreshing a data culture in an organisation requires a concerted effort that involves a combination of leadership support, training, and creating an environment that encourages the use of data in decision-making.

It may require a programme of activity over a number of years however, whilst you will need leadership support, thoroughly engaged stakeholders, lots of know-how, knowledge transfer and training / learning support, that may well not be your starting point!

Just for clarity, let's just ensure we understand the difference between programmes and projects. These definitions are taken from *"Managing Successful Programmes"* (MSP) and broadly generally accepted, although edited a bit to fit our graphic.

Programme Definition "MSP / generally accepted."	• Work to co-ordinate, direct, oversee the implementation of multiple projects / components, to deliver outcomes and benefits for strategic objectives. • May last several years, over multiple phases. often around distinct step changes in capability / benefit realisation

Project Definition "MSP / generally accepted."	•Usually temporary, for a shorter duration, delivers one or more outputs alinged to an agreed business case.

To be honest, we don't care that much about the exact definitions. **In our view what is important is, a commitment to Data is not short term thing!**

So, irrespective of the initiative term you use, be clear that once you start this ball rolling, it will pick up speed. And with the right people, resources, support, incentives, and hopefully with a bit of LUCK, it will deliver the outcomes you desire.

And we all know what L.U.C.K is don't we? ☺

Key Message

L.U.C.K is:

Labour - Under - Correct - Knowledge!

Key Message 15 - LUCK is Labour under correct knowledge.

Just to remind you of a few of our key messages and TNT's so far:

* When you assume, you make an ass out of you and me.

- Keep it simple.
- Data always exists.
- Know why!
- If it isn't broken, don't fix it.
- Change is not easy.
- Projects fail, because of people and resources.
- Failing to plan is planning to fail.
- Garbage in, garbage out.
- You can't build on shifting sand.

These are all "steps" to consider and act on.

But fundamentally, you're probably reading this because you're interested in the subject and maybe (hopefully) because you want to deliver some positive data culture change outcomes. So, again,

"Change will not come if we wait for some other person or some other time. We are the ones we've been waiting for. We are the change that we seek." (Barack Obama)

Or to edit Art Williams, "*Just get on and do it*"!

We're going to discuss some of the Key steps you can take but first, we want to offer up a simple framework to get you thinking. We call it the VIPP framework:

Figure 12 - Our VIPP framework.

What is the purpose of my organisation? What are we here to do? Who do we do it for? Why do we do it? Do we do it differently from others? Are we better at it? Where do I fit?

What are the problems we have in achieving our purpose? What could / should / must we do better?

What are our ideas for improvement? Do they pass the so what test? Are they of value? Can we do them?

Do we have a big picture vision, yet? Don't fret if not. Deal with what you can first.

Another way of using the VIPP model is to focus / ask: "*OK people, what are the very important points, that we must not miss?*"

Use it whichever way you prefer or use your own approach.

What's important is to get clarity in answering these questions. But remember, **clarity doesn't mean certainty**.

Like much of what we say, adapt it to fit if that helps. Tip - If you're just starting out or aren't sure yet of the vision, then start small!

And remember that people may engage with this differently, depending on where they fit within the organisation. A ship has a captain, officers and a crew. They could well see things differently. You may well need to use language that fits with your audience!

Tips 'n Techniques (TNT) 13 - Start small.

You could undertake a RACI based stakeholder engagement as indicated earlier, or you could just start much closer to home. Apply it to your team or department first perhaps. For example if you start in your own area of control / influence then you don't need to even adopt the philosophy of Seek forgiveness not permission. You can just do it, can't you? Discuss with your team first perhaps. Or a great topic for an away day.

Put your own house in order first?

So if you're a Chief Data Officer, what do you control, are responsible for?

If you haven't done so already, think about and document your responsibilities. Get it on a side of A4! Your job description might help, however that might be part of the problem. Probably worth dusting it off first though. See what it contains, as perhaps as importantly what it doesn't. Have you agreed any personal objectives either directly for data culture or indirectly where it plays a part?

In Berry's case, the purpose of UK police forces is something like *"Protecting life and property, preserving order, preventing offences, bringing offenders to justice"*. And even though her main executive sponsor has left, the brief was *"to make better use of data"*.

Some of the specific data culture challenges such as leadership support, lack of resources, and resistance to change are likely to apply for many types of change initiative. Berry might also currently be unable to address other organisation wide challenges like siloed data or data literacy. However data quality and data security are things she has a vested interest in. Within her own sphere of influence / her team she needs to find out if there is resistance to change and if there are data quality / literacy / security issues and also what she can do with the resources she has.

Whatever she does, she also knows it's better to:

Key Message

Under promise, over deliver

Key Message 16 - Under promise, over deliver.

We know that Berry has a vested interest in data quality and data security. So let's turn to DAMA, the Data Management Association for some help. They suggest things like the following to understand and assess data quality.

Dimension	Dimension Description
Accurate	Equal to real life value?
Complete	All mandatory values present? All optional but implied values present?
Consistent	Do data repositories align?
Current	Is data fresh, when compared to real world?
Precision	Is there enough detail?
Privacy	Does the data need restriction or monitoring?
Reasonable	Are current values in line with previous values?
Referential Integrity	Do child records have a parent?
Timely	Difference between when data is needed and when it is available
Unique	Does value occur just once within a dataset?
Valid	Within the expected format, range, data type, pattern etc for domain bounds?

Figure 13 - Data Dimension examples.

So, if Berry worked with her team, using even just some of these dimensions, she'd have an idea of whether, the data she holds, controls and is responsible for, is accurate, current, secure and valid? And in working with her team she'd be building up a sense of literacy, resistance and what pace of change might be achieved with the right resources?

If **she used *the VIPP framework*** to understand her fit with the force's purpose, followed just some of our earlier advice, like **passing the *so what*** test, she'd have some evidence (data!) which would show, assuming her pilot was representative across her organisation, what potential issues / problems might exist organisation wide?

Berry knows some just rely on their instincts and/or are not bought into data culture. Say she finds potential security issues, and/or that there is enough inaccurate data. Even the most sceptical stakeholders would probably concede that security could be a concern, or that working around or correcting inaccurate data is wasted effort. She might even find she starts to convert some!

After all:

Key Message
Seeing is believing

Key Message 17 - Seeing is believing.

We're great believers in seeing is believing. But you might need to start small to sell the ultimate vision.

Now, let's say Berry finds lot of issues in her own area. She probably ought to fix some of these first. Although there's a fine line between this and not sharing that there might be wider endemic issues which may have far worse implications for others.

Firstly though:

Tips 'n Techniques (TNT) 14 - More haste, less speed.

Let's recap. At this stage, Berry has, done some digging, found she's got some problems of her own, thinks there's an impact link to the organisation's purpose and that it's worth doing something about. She actually doesn't yet necessarily know what the answers (initiatives / solutions) could be, whether it's do-able or whether it's the right priority.

So even if it's just for the purposes of stakeholder engagement, we'd suggest **it's prudent to offer up some sensitivity analysis thoughts** and/or some proportionality thoughts. In simple words **apply some**

sensible what if projections. There's clearly an organisational culture link here.

Depending on how well she knows her audience, organisational culture, she can judge whether, for example it's better to say: *"what if the amount of what I've found is only 50% or 25% of what I've experienced, is it still a concern?"* Or *"what if it's twice?"*

Tips 'n Techniques (TNT) 15 - Ask what if?

Or she could turn it into a question, *"if our desired change outcomes are impacted by* [insert consideration factor], *is it still a concern / is there still enough value in doing it?".*

If you prefer the proportionality way of considering things *"when considered against abc, how much does xyz matter to you".*

Remember your change outcomes are likely to be related to your version of the **common drivers for change**. E.g. money, risk, strategy and so on.

So if, for example, one of your change outcomes was an increase/decrease of £50,000; the question might be, *"if, for whatever reason, we only made 50% or 25% of that income increase / cost decrease, would it still be worth doing?"*

It's often a good idea to consider macro relating factors that could influence outcomes. Remember you're dealing with **senior people; they often deal in headlines**.

Economic factors like this might include interest rates, inflation, prices of goods, supply shortages, competitive disrupters. You could throw in more organisational factors like user adoption, or delivery timescales too to get the debate going.

But let's also remember, *"No data, Is data"*! Berry might not have found much wrong in her own area. That's still data, evidence. What that probably means is that her house is in order; so, any issues or opportunities might lie elsewhere, or do they? That may well depend on what is, or perhaps should be, in her own house?

What's in your own house?

We said at the outset that this book is for business or technology leaders who are looking to use their organisations most strategic asset, their data, to drive value.

We also said that things just are not the same from organisation to organisation, department to department, team to team, person to person. In regards roles and responsibilities this means that people's roles and responsibilities will inevitably differ from organisation to organisation and so on.

We also said you could start by interviewing a representative group of stakeholders / users and building your own RACI model. In other words **find out what others think they are responsible for and what they think you are responsible for**! We're not trying to tell you what you should and shouldn't be responsible for. Just that getting clarity of that is helpful.

However, aside from perhaps the more general things (e.g. leadership support, change resistance, lack of resources etc.) here follows a simple list of **data roles and responsibilities** things that organisations are trying to grapple with and are lodged here for your consideration. It's not intended to be exhaustive and we're sure it will change / grow:

- Data quality
- Data literacy
- Data security
- Data management
- Data strategy
- Data analytics
- Data architecture
- Data integration
- Data governance
- Data democratisation
- Data science
- Data ethics

- Value / revenue generation
- Transformation
- Data culture

Once again, by all means take what we've noted and adapt and edit it to suit your own circumstances.

A core framework for change

We said at the outset that *"there's loads of helpful information, definitions, strategies, tactics, top tips, guides, frameworks, graphs freely available out there to help"*. We also said that *"one size doesn't fit all"* and *"backing one horse is higher risk"*. Balancing that we also said that *"we'll provide simple, effective frameworks that work"*.

There is one model though that we constantly use. That's not to say that we follow it religiously, we do right size it as we go. One way or another, 9 times out of 10, this is at the core of what we use ourselves to deliver. It is the *Lippitt-Knoster model for managing complex change*. We'll come back to it later on too but for now here's one, slightly simplified. version:

Vision	Agreement	Skills	Benefits	Resources	Action		Outcomes
✓	✓	✓	✓	✓	✓	→	Success

Figure 14 - Lippett - Knoster summary level.

104

We'll come back to each of these as we go through the key steps. Suffice to say though:

If you intend to make your data driven journey a success, you need to address all of these. Failing to manage even one, can lead to failure!

The following are the key steps needed to make your data-driven journey a success. Whether you should start with establishing leadership support though depends on you, your organisation, your relative data culture maturity compared with the outcomes you need and so on.

Establish leadership support.

Establish leadership support: **You believe that being data driven is the way forwards**. So from your perspective, the leadership of the organisation needs to actively support the idea of a data-driven culture. They need to understand the value of data and make it a priority for the organisation to collect, analyse, and use data to make informed decisions.

That doesn't mean they are going to see it the same way that you do or talk about it using the same language you do! In order to establish any support from outside of your domain, you must think about your audience. Use their terms, their words. If they want to get behind the words data driven culture, happy days! If they want to talk about business intelligence, so what, that's fine too. If they talk about customer retention or better cost control, great! That's making it real for them. It's not their job to embrace or translate that into the words data driven culture, if that's needed, that's yours!

You need to know your audience.

Tips 'n Techniques (TNT) 16 - Know your audience.

And you need to win their hearts and minds.

Key Message 18 - You need to win hearts and minds.

Berry currently doesn't have a project sponsor, he's left. She either needs to sponsor this herself or find an executive sponsor. Clearly this question is inherently linked with seniority, influence, roles and responsibilities that we have discussed previously. But unless Berry's on the leadership team, she is limited by how broad her own influence and control reaches.

Or is she?

We'll get to that.

Referencing the Lippitt-Knoster summary level above, to establish leadership support, at the simplest way of saying it, you almost certainly need 3 things:

- A vision
- Agreement / consensus
- A sponsor

Yes, those leaders will also want to know that the organisation has enough of the right skills, that the benefits are achievable, the resources are available and that it can successfully execute the required actions to deliver the outcomes. But fundamentally, there needs to be a vision, that they are agreed upon with some focused leadership (sponsorship).

You might wish to revert back to the section *"Building a data driven culture, where to start?"* to refresh some key messages, however there is one other thing that explicitly or perhaps more likely implicitly, that you will need to show to get the support of your executives and wider stakeholders. There's an obvious clue in the mentioned section. Before we get to it, we'll just quickly discuss the above.

Firstly, vision is everything. It should be directly related to the problems you're trying to solve (or opportunities you're trying to reach).

Tips 'n Techniques (TNT) 17 - Vision is everything.

Your vision is a compelling picture of the future that aligns stakeholders around the purpose of the initiative / project / change. As a result its benefits need to be clearly articulated so that your organisation can buy into the need for change.

Remember our number 1 key message? Start with why.

Your vision delivers to your why. It's what to your why.

Well actually that's not quite right, because what is perhaps better described as the strategy to deliver the vision, the goals if you prefer. However we quite like the "what to your why" aide memoire. And as you've found out, we're not that big on exact definitions, much preferring the simplicity of things being easy to remember, to get things done.

But watch out, if you don't have a vision, you 'll quickly reach confusion.

Key Message

A lack of vision leads to confusion.

Key Message 19 - A lack of vision leads to confusion.

And furthermore as we note, it needs to be compelling, its benefits need to be clear, easy to understand, straightforward to convey, so that people readily buy into it. Remind yourself of our VIPP model if you feel that helps you.

You may recall earlier we suggested that we said - *"The best place to start to understand your why, is to start to understand what the problems are you are trying to solve".* We've advised you to write things down too! So if you had the sorts of problems that our earlier wording noted, maybe your vision would look something like this?

> "Our vision (goal) is to improve our understanding of our customers, why and how they engage with us and to reduce the amount errors and re-work correcting them, so that we can significantly improve our customer services, destress our own daily working lives and deliver what matters to our customers the most.
>
> We will deliver a range of data capture, creation, analysis and management best practice advice,

training and solutions to help all of us understand our customers better and perhaps where we unknowingly get things wrong".

We're not saying ignore our earlier key messages of asking:

- So what?
- Is it worth it?
- Is it do-able?

Your executive / leadership team will want to know these answers too! Whether the evidence you present to them needs to be conveyed to wider stakeholder and user groups as a further part of the vision is down to you.

We're sure you could critique our example vision and make it better and/or simpler:

> "Our vision (goal) is to improve our understanding of our customers, so that we can improve our customer services and deliver what matters the most".

The 2nd "*we will deliver*" paragraph is not really a vision statement. It's more detail on how you'll deliver it. For many it's probably not needed. For some, that level of detail may help with engagement? It's all influenced by your organisational culture.

Your vision has to fit you, your organisation, your culture.

As previously noted, it might be a good idea to engage a representative group to consider what the vision should be, and to perhaps run an early stage proof of concept, even before a pilot, to test out how compelling, understandable and engaging it is alongside some of the sorts of things you're thinking of delivering so you can assess adoption too.

Then secondly, to establish support, what needs to happen? People need to agree. Consensus (as Lippitt-Knoster called it) has to be established.

In organizations today, it's very difficult for a leader to push through change without first gaining consensus - and this is where having a grasp of the bigger picture comes in.

Knowing how the wider plan fits together and how it will deliver your vision is crucial if you want others to share your beliefs. There is power in consensus.

Part of the challenge with gaining agreement is of course for people to buy into - do we need this? **Part of it is - can we, do it?**

And then there is also **should we do this**, alongside everything else we're doing at the moment.

The latter part of that is really about prioritization. Prioritization is not really a subject we're trying to advise upon here. However, there are key messages that could help you. For example, knowing the value of the problems you can solve would be one. And if you focus on doing the right things, you're surely improving your chances of your initiative being prioritized.

If people don't agree with you, they aren't incentivized to help you!

Key Message

A lack of agreement leads to sabotage!

Key Message 20 - A lack of agreement leads to sabotage.

We're not saying that people deliberately set out to sabotage your initiative. But, just as an example, if you're relying on a key individual in a different directorate / department to help you at a key stage, and that person simply doesn't do what you expect them to do, it could well be because they have other priorities. They may not be thinking they are sabotaging your initiative. They are though deliberately doing something else. Their deliberate inaction for you, is impacting you, potentially destroying what you're trying to do.

Ultimately though, we cannot tell you what you should be prioritizing and what you shouldn't bother with. Only you and your organization can decide that. However, if you do have an executive level sponsor in mind, they would probably have a decent idea of whether this is a priority? If it wasn't they probably wouldn't be interested in sponsoring it!

112

What's the typical role of a project sponsor:

Sponsor's Role - key examples
- Purpose, Value, Direction of project
- Provides resources / removes barriers
- The Main Champion
- Links to Big Picture / Strategy
- Project Oversight

Figure 15 - Role of a Project Sponsor

This is not a detailed book about project sponsorship, so let's keep things simple. **Your project sponsor is the main driver and needs to have skin in the game**! (Also true for your key supporters).

Key Message

Skin in the game is vital

Key Message 21 - Skin in the game is vital.

Berry doesn't currently have an executive sponsor and she's not on the leadership team. So she needs to find one. She knows that a number of key senior stakeholders are at best ambivalent to becoming data driven, and at worst anti it.

She's tried to understand who fits in where. It wasn't easy. Frankly at this point, her data roles and responsibilities RACI, is at best a work in progress. But that's ok. She made a plan. She spoke with some target stakeholders. She gathered some data. She now knows clearly where she stands with some. However there are some possible supporters and perhaps if she can find the right examples, she could find someone willing to sponsor. If she didn't know this before, she's fully realised that this will be a marathon not a sprint. Berry's is fine with that. She wants to make a difference.

Tips 'n Techniques (TNT) 18 - Change is a marathon, not a sprint.

Thinking about what Berry has uncovered so far and considering things at a big picture level. She knows, as with most organisations, payroll costs i.e. how many people, are near or at the top of the cost base for the organisation. She doesn't want to make redundancies, that doesn't feel like the right thing. She's found however that like many forces, they are short of people. There are a number of vacancies across many departments. So there's something here.

At this point she's not yet ready to approach her leaders with her big idea. She needs to flesh things out more. She will though put her own house in order, there were a few niggling things that weren't quite right. This will also give her some time to bed these fixes in with her team, learn how to bring her influence to bear, and prove that even if it's just in her area, she is delivering.

If you though, are at the point where timing is right, and you have a decent idea of why you need to do something, and what you can do about it, note, dealing with executives / senior leaders often isn't easy. So here are a few know-how tips.

- **Give them a decision to make**, otherwise they will be frustrated. *"What was the point of that"* they might well think or say afterwards.

- **Plans not products**. Senior people often say they take the longer term view. **Sell them a plan**, not a shrink wrapped product.

- **They like to contribute.** Sometimes you need to deliberately leave things out (even if you know the answer!). Or a middle ground; why not give them options? E.g. *"I was wondering, for user adoption, should we lead with the benefits to the organisation or to them"?*

- **Think policy, not procedure**. They (and their people) might be doing things because of the current policy. Draw attention away from how they are currently doing things.

- **Seeing is believing.** Their attention span is generally pretty short. So don't overdo the evidence detail, the solution demo's etc. Just enough, is enough!

- **You're the expert.** They are unlikely to be "Data professionals", more likely to be amateurs, but don't stress that! They will probably want to know "what good looks like", i.e. what should our decision criteria be? You should seed that into your discussions.

- **Know your audience!** As best as you can. What do your main drivers for change translate into? Apply the *"so what"* test. E.g. Data driven decision making, could give us competitive edge? Reducing data quality errors, reduces re-work costs but could improve Customer Satisfaction? If you're more unsure of how they will react, this is a great area to ask them about.

- **People buy from people they know**. Consider your level of influence. If you haven't been there long, don't bite off more than you can chew! You will probably need support from someone.

- **Keep your team involved and on side.** They might get asked by a leader they know.

- **Senior executives often seek organisational change**. They like to say, "*I did that*". They also will have objectives themselves to deliver. How can you help? Can you align with them?

Summarizing what you need for leadership support, you need:

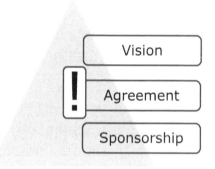

Tips 'n Techniques (TNT) 19 - You need vision, agreement, sponsorship.

And be prepared!

Tips 'n Techniques (TNT) 20 - You never get a second chance to make a first impression.

How to establish leadership support

When you think about building a data-culture, and gaining buy-in from the organisation leadership, ask yourself this:

> "Do people really want a data culture or do they really want the benefits that it can bring?"

It's probably the later, so when trying to sell this to the leadership sell them benefits and solutions to their problems that a data-driven culture will bring. Establishing leadership support for a data culture is crucial in building an organisation that values data and uses it to make informed decisions.

Once again, you'll find if you look, lots of great advice out there about asking questions and engaging people such as asking open questions not closed ones (i.e. don't ask those which prompt a yes / no response) and learning to switch off your own views and really just listen to the answers.

"We have two ears and one mouth, for a reason, to listen first!" (Anonymous)

Or paraphrasing a bit another quote:

"Seek to understand before you seek to be understood." (Stephen Covey)

By now though you have probably understood that one of our top pieces of advice is to **seek clarity**, in everything that you do. Remember clarity isn't certainty.

And as a top technique for discussing things with your stakeholders, gaining clarity, is one of, if not the best investigation, analysis, and assessment aide memoires to keep in mind near the forefront of your engagement and analysis approach.

"I keep six honest serving men (they taught me all I knew); Their names are What and Why and When and How and Where and Who." (Rudyard Kipling)

And if you remember that he also wrote *"If"*, then you can engage further with your stakeholders and determine their level of need fulfilment with your proposed solution.

"If we delivered xyz, how much benefit would you receive"?

Another perhaps equally **great technique is "5 Whys"**. This was invented by Sakichi Toyoda of the Toyota Motor Company, also instrumental in LEAN theory and method. Its intention is to get to the root cause of things. Or in our words, to get clarity. The principle is to repeat the question why, 5 times, until you've dug down enough to get to the truth. WARNING! Simply asking Why 5 times, may well rub those you're trying to engage with up the wrong way! As we've said similarly elsewhere, don't fixate on the definition, just use the principle where it makes sense.

There are several approaches you can take to establishing leadership support, you may find you use a blend of all of these:

Build personal relationships with members of the senior leadership team. These relationships can help the CDO gain support for their initiatives and identify potential roadblocks before they become major issues.

How would you do that? Probably depends on how long you've been around, where you fit and so on, and frankly this might be a bit obvious, you need to go and speak with them! Don't just assume!

Revisit our ***How do I start*** section. Find out what their problems are, if / where they see their fit within a data roles and responsibilities model, speculate (i.e. test out) how something you could do, in and around data, might help them.

When you're engaging with anyone you might find it helpful to express your questions or your thoughts in different ways.

As data analysis professionals should know, if you triangulate the views of the data, i.e. you look at it from multiple (e.g. 3) different lenses, and you basically get the same answer, confidence in the analysis and judgement grows i.e. it's pretty likely to be right.

If you **ask people the same question a different way around,** maybe you'll get the same answer, if so great! And if you get a different answer, great! That's just more views, evidence, data you need to consider.

If you say, don't feel the answer to the question feels quite right, or you feel there's more to it than meets the reply, ask / say basically the same thing, but a different way around. Try it, it works!

Partly as an example, partly to inject some humour!

Gethyn / Mark (Us): *"Have you found the advice in this book useful to you"?* (We know it's a closed question, a yes / no answer, bear with us, you can use them too).

You: *"Yes I have"*.

Us: " *Great". "What have you used and how have you used it"?*

You: *"Oh I really like the simplicity of know-why and so what. When I spoke with the operations director the other day, I found the six honest serving men questions really helpful in us jointly getting clarity of the issues and problems that exist"*.

Us: *"That's fabulous". "Why didn't you use the 5 why's technique"?*

You: *"Oh I like that too. It's also useful. I just didn't need it at that point"*.

Us: *"Why not"?* (Ok so that's one too many why's perhaps in this case but you get the idea, don't you?)

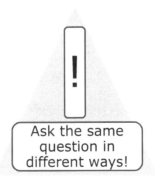

Tips 'n Techniques (TNT) 21 - Ask the same question in different ways.

And in building those relationships, here's a couple of quick do's and don'ts.

Do listen and be respectful to their views. It's how they see things after all. That doesn't mean that you can't challenge, or perhaps more softly, subtly suggest a different viewpoint. They might agree or disagree with it. Either way you're gathering more information, more data to consider.

Don't get too purist about the technicalities of whether something is data / data culture etc. through your expert eyes. They won't care. All you're seeking is a relationship that might help you in the future.

Don't forget though that if you say you'll do something for them, *under promise and over deliver*! You will have to fight very hard to get a second chance from a first impression!

Demonstrate the value of data: Start by demonstrating to your leaders the value of data and its potential to impact the organisation. Use case studies, industry research, and data-driven examples to illustrate how data can help the organisation make better decisions, optimize operations, and drive growth.

Did you have anything to put right in your own house? What did it do for you? What might something similar do for them? Skip forwards, have a look at the sections of *Build a data-driven mindset* and *Nurture with nature*. Bring that evidence, that data, back into your leadership / stakeholder engagement.

Demonstrate quick wins: Demonstrating quick wins is an effective way to build momentum and gain support for data initiatives. A CDO should identify low-hanging fruit where data can be used to achieve quick wins, quick wins mean benefit to the business and then communicate these successes to the leadership team.

Don't get hung up on whether the quick win fits a data vision or not. Frankly you may not be anywhere near knowing what that vision is yet? Many so called transformation programmes fail to deliver expected results, thus disappointing customers, operational teams and wider stakeholders precisely because the expectations are set too early!

If your quick win is successful, you'll have made some improvements and it will give you credibility. Your next request for change is more likely to be viewed favourably as your Leadership knows you can deliver.

If you've already sold that you're "solving all the world's problems" and your further analysis (remember *plan, do, check, act)* suggests some minor changes, expectations will have been set, things you've said may be hard to take back and could lead to frustration and disappointment.

Develop a clear vision and data strategy: Develop a clear data strategy that outlines the benefits of a data culture and how it aligns with the organisation's overall goals. We keep repeating this alongside gaining agreement to it because it is it vital!

Relevant to this here's a reminder of a few of these key messages and TNT's so far:

- Know why!
- Data culture aligns with organisational culture.
- Do the right things.
- Break things down.
- Start small.
- Plan - Do - Check - Act
- Under promise - Over deliver
- Seeing is believing.
- You need to win hearts and minds.

These are all steps to consider and act on, not necessarily in one go. Remember what senior people like. They like plans, they like the big picture but they also like to contribute and to make decisions. Isn't it likely to be much easier for you to get a decision on something smaller whilst you're building up to the big plan?

So yes, your plan should, at some point, include a roadmap for implementing a data culture and the steps needed to achieve it. But don't make it too fixed to begin with, even if you truly know what is going to happen. Chances are something will happen that you have no control over, and you'll need to change a bit. Predicting the future isn't easy! You may well need time and some more data to develop that vision and the associated roadmap of deliverables.

Let's also just talk quickly about differences between vision and strategy. Your strategy is not, to become the number 1 provider of widgets in your sector. That could be your vision, although in that case, that's always likely to be a tall order and, what does that mean if someone else does it? You'd fail, despite perhaps materially increasing / improving stuff. Maybe your vision should have a broader interpretation, permit a bit more leeway. Your strategy though is what you are going to do, how you are planning to reach that goal, your vision.

We talked earlier about our VIPP model, vision, idea, problem, purpose. If it sits better in your culture to simply focus on the very important points, do that! The way we've shown it is with purpose at the top of the wheel, i.e. to be clear and understand what your organisation's purpose, your department's (and ultimately your own) purpose is. It could equally be vision at the top. We're not that fussed.

However we do recognise that your organisation may well already have a vision that is well established or indeed being rolled out. As we've previously noted, we're not fixated on exact definitions the important point is to get things done. Please don't get hung up on what the difference between vision and purpose is. If you have got one, that'll do. If you have got both, happy days. Either are a starting place.

In some sectors purpose might be more obvious. In the Public and Not for profit sectors, organisations are set up explicitly to do certain things; Provide housing, education, vulnerable persons support and so on. It's then up to that organisation to decide what their vision is for helping those vulnerable people in need.

In others, maybe it's vision? Now if we looked back at say Amazon, what were their origins? It doesn't matter if this example is 100% correct or not, it's the thoughts we're trying to promote. Googling it now, suggests that their mission / vision was to be earth's most customer-centric company. OK, it may well have been. Our experience was that they seemed to set out to sell books and CD's, cheaper and better than others. So maybe their vision or their purpose was to be the most customer centric company, and their strategy was to start small, with books and CD's. And maybe phase 2 of their roadmap for books was the e-reader that you may well be reading this e-book on.

Who knows? What's vital is that you align your data culture strategy to one or the other or both. And wherever you are within your organisation, a really

126

great way to make that VIPP model real for you is to know exactly where you and others fit to align to the purpose.

If I'm the CDO, what is my purpose to help the organisation achieve its purpose, its vision. Identify that golden thread that runs through the entire organisation.

Tips 'n Techniques (TNT) 22 - Find the golden thread.

Perhaps when you're doing your data roles and responsibilities map, you could ask stakeholders where their place on that golden thread is? In other words:

> "*If you* [insert department] *didn't do xyz" what would be the impact for the organisation?* And then,

> "*What else* [insert department] *could you do to improve this if you also knew abc?*"

You know we like to tell a story to help get the message across. Perhaps you could do the same. It doesn't have to be a story as such, it could be a mind map, a roadmap, or just a set of simple easy to convey / easy to understand goals. Storyboards though, particularly at the user engagement end, are a great way of making it real, of visualising it. After all:

A picture paints ten thousand words.

Key Message

A picture paints ten thousand words.

Key Message 22 - A picture paints ten thousand words.

You want, no, you need, people to engage. They need things they can remember, easily.

Develop a business case: A CDO should develop a business case for how data can help the organization achieve its goals. The business case should highlight the potential return on investment and the long-term benefits of a data-driven approach.

Do I need a
business
case?

Or should they?

Check back to our **What problems am I trying to solve** section and the **Common drivers for change** in particular. These should help you with the basics. Use some of our key messages and TNT's such as:

- Ask so what - this might do or improve, that relates to your purpose , your vision.

- Ask what if - key internal and external factors change, and this might mean for your argument, your case.

- Apply proportionality - for its relative priority to other things.

- Know you can do it.

Whatever you do, don't simply knock on the door of the powers that be, before you've signposted your thoughts and gained some level of traction, some buy in. The business case is perhaps more the evidence / the data to support the decision, than it is that which wins their hearts and minds.

By way of an example to perhaps show both why business cases are and maybe aren't needed:

Many years ago in the UK we had a nationalised rail service, British Rail. It was privatised in 1993. It was divided up into over 100 different companies. And there was a problem. (Well there were many frankly; this was one Mark was directly involved in at BT plc).

The problem, for the passenger Train Operating Companies (TOC's), i.e. the ones running the trains, providing the service of getting people from a to b, was passengers (customers) could not get through on the telephone to the Telephone Enquiry Bureaus (TEBs). They were constantly getting the engaged tone.

The engaged tone is not perhaps so prevalent today but back then it was a fairly common outcome of trying to get through to people on the phone. But just like today, people wanted information on what time the trains were running, how much the ticket was, how long it took, was there parking at the station and so on. This was long before the modern internet enabled world and contact centres as we know them now.

Basically lots and lots and lots of people were complaining! And that was bad press as well as (very) poor customer service, let alone potentially lost revenues. The government, regulator, unions, the TOC's executives, staff wanted an answer.

But what was the issue? To get clarity on the problem, (the root cause) if you asked the TEB managers what the data from their telephony systems said, quite often that data showed that most of the calls were being answered!

Not in all cases, but there was enough opinion that said *"we don't know (or see) the problem, we're answering as many calls as we get. We can't do any more".*

And yet, lots and lots of people were complaining they couldn't get through.

Surely both facts (we're answering all the calls we get / callers can't get through) couldn't both be right, could they?

Well, actually there was truth in both. Let us explain.

It was true that the TEB managers data showed that "their telephony systems / agents" were answering lots of calls. It was also true that passengers were getting the engaged tone, lots of times.

Using the 5 Why's technique.

> "Why / how can callers get an engaged tone and yet the calls answered data shows most calls answered"?

The answer lay in the data!

The TEB managers could only see the data that they could see. In other words, they:

> "Couldn't see what they couldn't see, they didn't know what they didn't know"!

The TEB systems could not identify and track the calls from the originating points (the caller's phone in their homes and offices) and through the network to their system. They could only see the data from the point at which their system started tracking it, i.e. when it was in their system.

But BT could! And back then (we don't know if this is done now) if there were more calls than could fit down however many lines that the TEB manager had bought to plug into their telephony answering system, BT presented the callers with the engaged tone.

So both facts were right. The issue was in correctly identifying the source of the problems.

Or in other words, the right people, with sufficiently inquisitive natures, asked the right questions, gathered and analysed the right data and found the right solutions to deliver the right outcomes.

In that case it was getting the vast majority (all) of the calls being answered. For what it's worth the right data showed that over 90% of initiated calls, were often getting the engaged tone! It was a wow moment for sure!

Bringing us back to the business case. Was one needed? Well yes it was. But it was developed!

Tips 'n Techniques (TNT) 23 - Develop your business case.

Documented discussions and presentations were undertaken with all of the stakeholders as above. Personal relationships were built.

This did take time; it was an industry that was being convinced after all! Some of those TOC's had already set up their own contact centres to sell tickets over the phone. So we had already established some evidence of a potential solution. Some quick wins or seeing is believing if you like.

The value of the data was obvious, and it was easy to convey a simple, clear vision of answering *all* calls with all the benefits of no more bad press, better customer service and more people buying tickets and travelling on the trains.

Almost everyone had skin in the game and hearts and minds were won over.

In truth, there were lots of small agreements (yes's) along the way.

Perhaps, it felt daunting for those involved and nerves were frayed whilst awaiting the business case decision. But the business case was doing the right thing! The why was clear, data evidenced the problems, solutions were developed, stakeholders were bought in and aligned.

We've said it's good practice to write things down and it is. So maybe that's all a business case is, a written document that makes things clear so that people can decide. So yes, it is needed. But maybe all the work should be done before and it's just the last step in building a successful data culture?

(Postscript: we could have used this example to highlight many steps in this book, like building a data driven mindset, nurturing with nature or overcoming resistance to change. So as we've said, use what works for you, wherever you feel it might add value).

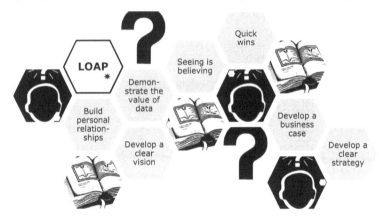

LOAP - Learning on a Page 5 - How to establish leadership support.

Key stakeholders in building a data driven culture.

It's imperative to identify the key people within the organisation who can benefit from using data to make decisions. This may include department heads, project managers, and other stakeholders who have access to data that can be used to make decisions.

Building a data-driven culture involves collaboration between different stakeholders in an organisation.

It is almost certain that there will be existing departments that already analyse data to provide information and recommendations. E.g.

Finance is in charge of figures! They have been producing Income / Profit & Loss statements, Balance sheets, Cash flow forecasts and so on for years.

Marketing is probably in charge of your website (and maybe digital) engagement. They already know how much website traffic there is.

Clearly you should be careful about treading on people's toes. You don't want to cause confusion and you don't want to develop road blockers or worse, enemies.

Furthermore ask yourself this: what is the value of delving into areas where data is already being used well to support decision making? That's just re-inventing the wheel. However:

- What don't they know?
- What would they like to know?
- Where would this come from?
- How valuable would it be?

Find something that isn't being measured and analysed.

Did you build your **data roles & responsibilities model?** If so great.

If not, maybe now's the time? If you've got to the stage where you're considering or are seeking Executive and Senior Stakeholder support for something that leads towards a vision, a strategy, then you will very likely need people's support, even if you are the CEO!

For example, in the UK there are legal data protection compliance requirements laid down by the Information Commissioners Office (ICO). Your regulatory regime may well have similar? For clarity, we are not claiming to be data protection experts, these are just examples intended to get you thinking. They should not be relied upon as factual or taken as advice in any way. You should consult your own legal advisors and experts.

Taking Subject Access Requests (SAR) and Freedom of Information requests (FOI) as the examples. Broadly these are requests that people may make to organisations for information. If your organisation receives one, they may then have to do something. (As things stand, broadly SARs typically apply to most entities holding / processing personal data and FOIs in general to public sector type organisations - note: consult your own legal advisors, experts).

In the UK, data protection law comprises the GDPR and the Data Protection Act 2018. Organisations were required to comply, and many put in a huge effort to become and / or re-assure themselves that they were compliant. But even if handling SARs and FOIs aren't your responsibility as CDO, surely you should at least know where data is (e.g. for SAR inquiry) and whether you're retaining it for longer than the required timeframes; and relevant stakeholders would therefore understand your interest. Do those already involved / responsible for SARs and FOIs have concerns? What might it mean for us, for you, for me? Should we do something about it? is it do-able? Is it worth it?

But be careful, if it's not your responsibility, it's not your responsibility to fix it either. People have a habit of thinking that a problem shared is suddenly now somehow not their problem! Apply the so what test, proportionality etc. with them, there might be bigger fish to fry. After all, in the UK your organisation was supposed to have done this a few years ago weren't they?

Berry has tried to engage some stakeholders to build her data roles and responsibilities model. It's still very much a work in progress though. She has discovered though, that there seems to be quite a lot of effort involved in responding to these requests, often with people being taken off front line duties to do so, as and when they come in.

You could also build a key stakeholder management map?

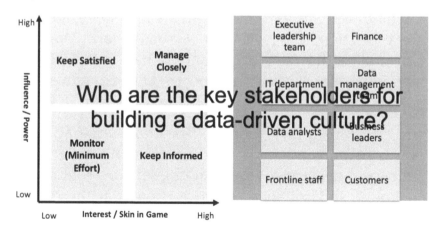

Figure 16 - Key Stakeholder management map for your data journey?

Your stakeholders may differ, but these are some to consider when working on your stakeholder map and working out a strategy to manage and work with the stakeholders.

Executive leadership: Executive leadership is critical in establishing a data-driven culture. They need to set the tone for the organisation by demonstrating their commitment to data-driven decision-making and ensuring that the necessary resources are available to support this culture.

Finance controls the income and expenditure. They produce the Income / Profit & Loss Statements, Balance Sheet, Cash Flow forecasts. They probably handle Payroll and assess / maintain business risk profiles. They are a key player in running and improving the business.

IT department: The IT department is responsible for providing the infrastructure and tools necessary for data collection, analysis, and visualisation. They can help ensure that the organisation has the necessary technology and infrastructure to collect, store, and analyse data.

Data management team: The data management team is responsible for managing data and ensuring its quality and accuracy. They can help ensure that data is consistent and reliable, which is essential for making informed decisions.

Data analysts: Data analysts are responsible for analysing data and providing insights that can inform decision-making. They can help identify patterns and trends in the data that can inform strategies and tactics.

Business leaders: Business leaders are responsible for driving growth and achieving organisational goals. They can use data to inform decision-making and optimize operations to achieve their objectives.

Frontline employees: Frontline employees interact with customers and have direct experience with the organisation's operations. They can provide valuable insights that can inform data-driven decision-making and help identify areas for improvement.

Customers: Customers are an important stakeholder in building a data-driven culture. By collecting and analysing data on customer behaviour and preferences, organisations can better understand their needs and deliver a better customer experience. Clearly, your sales, marketing and operational teams and departments will inevitably have regular touch points with our customers.

Building a data-driven culture requires collaboration between different stakeholders in an organisation. By working together, these stakeholders can create a culture that values data-driven decision-making and uses data to drive growth and improve outcomes. Sometimes you might feel that getting all of the stakeholders to work together is a bit like herding cats. Which is why it's important that you have buy in from the very top of the organisation who can set the tone and expectations of what is needed.

The figure above shows a typical stakeholder management model. It shows what to manage. It doesn't show how to engage, manage the people though. We'd like to go one step further and suggest a method to use when in discussions with stakeholders. We call it our "PR" model.

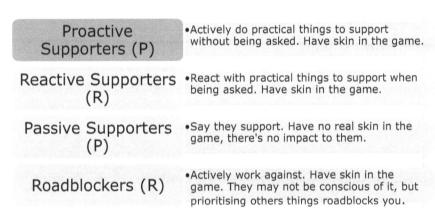

Proactive Supporters (P)	•Actively do practical things to support without being asked. Have skin in the game.
Reactive Supporters (R)	•React with practical things to support when being asked. Have skin in the game.
Passive Supporters (P)	•Say they support. Have no real skin in the game, there's no impact to them.
Roadblockers (R)	•Actively work against. Have skin in the game. They may not be conscious of it, but prioritising others things roadblocks you.

Figure 17 - Our PR model.

Clearly when you're in discussions with your stakeholders you can and should ask them whether they support your initiative or not, and they will hopefully answer. Whilst that's fine, is that really evidence, can it be relied upon, or is it "*not worth the paper it's written on*"?

Warning: Don't disregard what we've already advised.

For example, if and what you do here needs to fit your style and the culture. It needs to meet a why. Maybe having undertaken an initial stakeholder survey you've some niggling stakeholder support related concerns that aren't quite sitting right for you. It needs to be worth it, do-able, timed appropriately. It needs to be proportionate.

Some of the techniques we've noted, such as asking:

"So what would this mean for you, how much of an impact might this have for you?" Or
"Why are you supporting this, why does it make a difference to you?",

and so on, could be used, carefully! You need to be careful how you do this. People might see this as a challenge to them and you don't want to poke them in the eye with a sharp stick. So think about your approach style, the breadth, depth of evidence you'd like and the words you use, if you feel this model can help you.

What you're trying to get to is to jointly gain agreement that they really do have skin in the game or not and hence whether it really helps them and you to be in contact too often. You also want to know whether you can rely on them to action whatever has been discussed and agreed. Delivery does not happen without actions.

If you analyse and then combine your Data Roles & Responsibilities model, with your Stakeholder Management Map and use the PR model to really understand where your support is and roadblocks are, you're on the way to having a plan aren't you? **You've got your As Is**?

But what else are you doing?

You're practicing what you preach!

Key Message

Practice what you preach

Key Message 23 - Practice what you preach.

You're acting, engaging with people, gathering data, doing some analysis, making some plans, some proposals. **You are just doing it!**

And if you use *Plan - Do - Check - Act, Measure Twice, Cut Once*, and *More Haste Less Speed*, you're likely increasing quality too.

Fundamentally you are showing you are using a data driven mindset yourself.

Build a data-driven mindset.

Educating employees on the importance of data is essential in building a data-driven culture in an organisation. It can help the employee build a data-driven mindset which can the influence their behaviour towards using data.

Here are some ways to educate employees on the importance of data:

Provide data literacy training: Offer training to employees that focuses on the basics of data, data analysis, and data visualisation. This training can be provided in the form of workshops, seminars, or e-learning modules.

Use data to demonstrate the impact: Use real-life examples to demonstrate the impact of data on the organisation. Show how data has been used to solve problems, make informed decisions, and drive growth. This can help employees see the value of data and motivate them to become more data-literate.

Make data accessible: Make data accessible to employees by providing them with access to data analysis and visualisation tools. This can help them see the data in a more tangible way and understand its potential to impact the organisation.

Encourage experimentation: Encourage employees to experiment with data and use it to test new ideas and approaches. This can help them become more comfortable with using data and build confidence in their ability to use data to drive growth and improve outcomes.

Develop data champions: Identify employees who are passionate about data and make them data champions. These champions can help to educate and inspire their colleagues to become more data-literate.

Educating employees on the importance of data is essential in building a data-driven culture in an organisation. Educate on the importance of data and its potential to impact the organisation. By providing training, making data accessible, and creating a data-driven culture, organisations can help their employees become more data-literate and use data to make informed decisions. Encourage them to think about how data can be used to solve problems, make informed decisions, and drive growth. This will help overcome resistance to change from sections of your workforce.

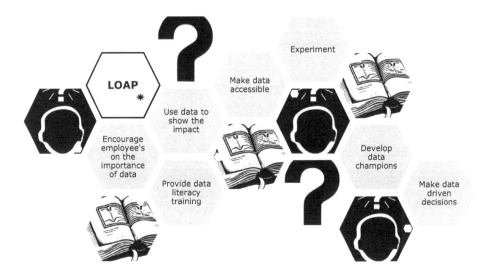

LOAP - Learning on a Page 6 - How to build a data driven mindset.

Nurture with nature

We said earlier that unless Berry was on the leadership team, she was perhaps limited by how broad her own influence and control reaches. Given that she's pretty new, it's also possible that even if she has a great idea, given how sceptical some of her colleagues appear to be, she may well find it difficult to get support when she asks for it. She could easily encounter resistance along the lines of *"how would she know; she's only been her 5 mins"*!

But there is one significant advantage that a CDO or just anyone interested in data, may have over other heads of department trying to get their initiatives off the ground. Let us explain.

It's generally accepted good practice, if it's a new project or a program that Berry would be trying to get off the ground, it would probably have a structure something like the following:

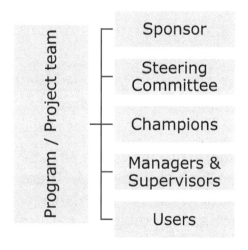

Figure 18 - Typical Program / Project Structure

Whatever the size of your organisation, as this is relative, that's a lot of people, a lot of structure to get established. If someone was trying to get a new CRM initiative off the ground, then they would probably have to have worked out their vision, their strategy, some of their solutions before asking for support from the leadership. Because they are likely to be asking for significant resources, i.e. time, money and effort to get it done. All of which would be on top of their existing "Business as usual"! Yes, they could perhaps then establish a pilot to prove they are heading in the right direction of travel. But fundamentally they are likely to have to do a lot of work upfront before they can evidence any progress, any improvement.

As and when Berry is ready to sell her ideas to the powers that be something along the above lines is, just like anything else, what she'll probably need. But does she have to be as bold or do as much upfront work, herself?

So, is she limited by how broad her own influence and control reaches? We said we'll get to this so here's our premise.

Leaders, managers and users are already working with and using data. Even the sceptics. There aren't many, if any, organisations, departments who don't review financial performance, employee performance, report mistakes or make business cases to invest for example. Granted whether these are extensively written down or not is driven by the legal regimes operated within and the culture of the organisation.

But, relating back to the *fear of change,* data isn't new! Berry isn't necessarily asking to do

something new; she may simply be stating what's needed to "Keep the Lights on" (KTLO).

If you don't already know of this model, we'd like to introduce you to our take on the 70-20-10 model. *We believe this should be attributed to Google* as a decade or so ago, we gather they used it to help employees understand how it was allocating its resources and projects.

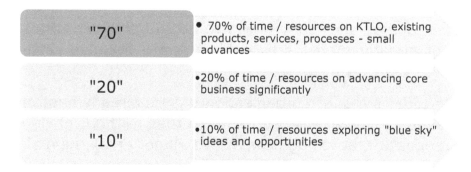

Figure 19 - A 70-20-10 focus model.

Perhaps unlike her Heads of Department peer group, **Berry doesn't need to start or focus on the 20 or the 10**?

She can, but **she could also likely find value in the 70. That's the area where everyone already is. It's the norm; people, time and money are already being used. She may not need to ask for or find that much additional investment.**

Once again, our view here is to not obsess about following the exact definition. If you spend all your time trying to fit your organisation exactly to the model, you won't have actually done anything! Apply the principles, use what works for you. Change the percentages, add a category if you wish. Remember though to Keep it simple. It's more likely to work.

Does Berry need to set up a new program or project structure to get her idea off the ground?

As stated, there will already be plenty of people already spending time, money and effort on the 70, as part of their business as usual.

Perhaps all she really needs to do to begin with if it's not already there, is to **set up some form of data interest community?**

In today's modern organisation there's already a lot of technology available to help with that, without having to invest in anything new. We've all got email, haven't we? And many have Microsoft Teams (or the equivalent of). And even if you haven't got Power BI, you almost as sure as eggs is eggs, have Excel (or its equivalent).

So, what's stopping you for just doing it?

If we break data down to perhaps its most simple. What is it / should it be about?

1. Input / Creation / Processing. There may not be enough of it, it may be being done well, or badly but it is being done already in the 70!
2. Analysis and reporting - remember don't step on other toes doing this already (such as with Finance, Marketing as discussed). Focus on things that aren't already being done.

148

3. Taking judgements / decisions on it.

As long as Berry and her team have enough time, to focus on doing some analysis and perhaps reporting (e.g. verbally back to her data community) and then facilitating some decisions, it's highly likely that someone in her data community will have benefitted in their current BAU. Berry will have her "*seeing is believing*", her pilot cases to evidence to the powers that be.

As an example, a division of a well-known UK financial services company, was trying to improve the skills of their existing change function. Budgets were tight. Explicit training budget allocation had to be in proportion to the rest of the budget. Which meant that there was never enough budget in any year to train people formally in any specific skill. E.g. a Business or Data Analysis course. Staff feedback consistently noted they wanted more investment in their skill development.

Some of that was that the employee wanted the badge or certificate that would enhance their CV. However much of it was that the people wanted to know that the firm was interested in them. Looking at the skill gaps, often they were more related not just to what a technique might be but how to apply the technique in practice. i.e. not just know what, but know-how. Formalised training courses often contained things that were either not very relevant, applicable to the individual or said person already knew it. In other words, there was an argument that the obvious solution (a formal training course) wasn't the best value for money.

The change leader formed their own People Development Forum. This comprised champions from the respective skill, across department areas (e.g. Project management, Business analysis, Data analysis, Development, Testing). The principle was to learn from each other, through various knowledge sharing activities, and decide where and who would benefit the most from a formal training course. The available budget was spent where it was needed. Visibility of the budget allocation rationale was related; staff saw fairness in it, and this further obtained buy in. Investment vs. performance vs. outcome data was gathered over time which was further used to improve on-going skill gaps.

It became self-managed and self-fulfilling. With very little actual investment (a small amount of BAU time), skills were improved, staff were happier and change deliverable outcomes improved. A happy by product was that formal training budget allocations also increased. Evidence of the investment in people was believed to be worth it.

In summary unless you're in a truly greenfield organisation, then:

- Data already exists (even when it doesn't, that's still data isn't it?) - in the "70".
- You can start small, and a small change could have a big impact.

The $64 million question is, what's the value in doing things better?

And you can find that out using nurture and nature.

Dealing with resistance to change

How do deal with the "This is how we do things around here" attitude. The resistance you encounter should be expected. You should proactively seek out the "objections". Don't let it shock you, hinder you or throw you off track of what you're doing. Write them down, discuss with the group, team or function who are showing resistance and work out your best strategy for dealing with them.

In our view, the very best way to deal with change is to start from the beginning. Paraphrasing Stephen Covey.

Key Message
Start with the end in mind

Key Message 24 - Start with the end in mind.

"Begin each day with a clear vision of your desired direction and destination, and then continue flexing your proactive muscles to make things happen." (Stephen Covey)

Let's break that down a bit. Do you want to set out to deal with resistance to change? Really? Surely not! However you probably do want to set out to engage your stakeholders and users. You don't really want to overcome resistance, ideally you want them to buy into the change - Carrot, not stick!

Track back to **How do I start** and/or to **A core framework for change** if you wish. In some ways they are saying the same sorts of things, albeit the language used is different. That's deliberate on our part. We don't know exactly who will be reading this and how they will feel about the different words we use. So we're offering different ways of saying similar things hoping that something will resonate and turn into something you can use.

If you set out to engage with clarity with your stakeholders and users, on why this change is right, how it's going to be done and how you'll ensure everyone will have what they need in good time for when things will happen, you'll be well on our way to gaining their buy in.

Remember your vision is a compelling picture of the future that aligns stakeholders around the purpose of the initiative. As a result, its benefits need to be articulated so that your organisation can buy into the need for change.

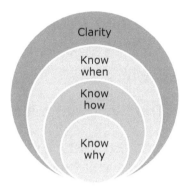

Figure 20 - Know why, how and when - clarity.

Why do people resist change?

"People don't resist change; they resist being changed." (Peter Senge)

We're not organisational psychologists, but we do have plenty of practical change experience. And Peter's quote resonates with us. Does it with you?

But if you don't believe us, google it, or seek out firms like Prosci (highly trusted and exclusively focused on change management) or respected commentators like Forbes, Harvard Business review and so on. You'll probably find that the following general headings appear pretty consistently. In our experience we've certainly come across these many times.

Examples of why people resist change:

- Lack of awareness of the reason for change.

- Clarity of the future direction and their security in it.

- They want to know-how to do it, changes in roles threaten their competence.

- Fear of the unknown.

- Lack of support from or trust in leaders.

- People want empowerment, they don't like being excluded from change related decisions.

And furthermore Prosci's *Best Practices in Change Management* research, consistently shows the following levels of change resistance from these broad groups:

- 9% Executives and Directors.
- 16% Senior Managers
- 42% Mid-level Managers
- 27% Front Line users

Maybe that helps to point out who to start with? Looking at this data the other way around, it also validates that Executives and Leaders don't fear change? Whilst from the data above, it would be wrong to conclude that 91% positively embrace change, there's a decent chance that many of that 91% do?

But in truth, the above data, information isn't important. What's important is what the situation is in your organisation, relating to the data culture initiative you believe needs to be done.

Put simply, you need to engage with your stakeholders, from the off.

"Start at the beginning, it's a very good place to start." (Julie Andrews / Rogers & Hammerstein!)

You need to engage. Provide context, start with why, ask how people feel about data, hold "future of data" workshops. Try a variety of these if you're unsure which might work best, if you know, use what you know works.

To repeat. You should proactively seek out the "objections". Don't let it shock you, hinder you or throw you off track of what you're doing. Write them down, discuss with the group, team or function who are showing resistance and work out your best strategy for dealing with them. As any good salesperson will tell you.

Objections are buying signals; they should be handled.

Tips 'n Techniques (TNT) 24 - Objections are buying signals.

Someone's *"objection"* is telling you what their concern is. If you can solve that, you have fulfilled their need! Keep in mind this old (customer) complaints adage:

"A happy customer tells a friend; an unhappy customer tells the world." (Unknown)

That said, it's almost inevitable that you will encounter some resistance at any stage, the start, middle and go live. How could you work out whether someone is likely to resist your change? One of the best user adoption techniques we've come across is:

What's in it for me?

Tips 'n Techniques (TNT) 25 - What's in it for me?

The basics are, from the viewpoint of the person you're engaging with, i.e. the user, department, key stakeholders, sponsor. What will the impact be for me? That could be positive, negative or in-between i.e. anything from "my life will be immeasurably easier to, my jobs at risk".

This can also be useful for engaging with senior stakeholders when seeking their support.

Examples of things you could discuss and work through in a "What's in it for me / you workshop"?

- What will things look like in the end?

- What might I need to give up?

- What will be new and different for me?

- What are the positives for me?

- What are the negatives for me and how could they be overcome?

- Are there any threats, how might they be mitigated?

- Which of these really matter?

There are lots of considerations for these including, the tasks they do, processes they use, skills they have / need, who's in the team, the ways of working, the environment they work in, priorities they have and so on. Be prepared to find out what should be considered and to explore them all. Remember,

> Perception can be reality.

Don't dismiss things because you don't think it's real.

It's a bit like doing a S.W.O.T analysis (Strengths, Weaknesses, Opportunities, Threats) and a "So what" assessment for the individuals and the departments involved.

If you need to explain what's going on? A great "communication" technique is:

- "WWW.com". What is the Change. Why is it happening? What's in it for you (& how we will avoid issues for you)? And the ".com" is all about communication. How are we communicating, keeping people informed etc.

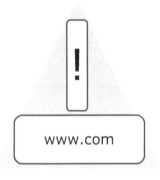

Tips 'n Techniques (TNT) 26 - www.com

It's all too easy to assume you think you know what it will mean.

You don't know! Not until you ask them! (Remember what the definition of assume is?)

Considering all of the above and if you wish using "what's in it for me" and/or "www.com" here's a summary of key steps for dealing with resistance to change:

Communicate the benefits: Communicate the benefits of a data culture and how it will help employees do their jobs better. This can help employees understand why the change is necessary and get them excited about the potential benefits. Perhaps even highlight the repercussions of not changing

Involve employees in the change process: Involve employees in the change process by seeking their input and feedback, and by encouraging them to participate in training and development opportunities. This can help employees feel more invested in the change and increase their willingness to adopt new practices.

Address concerns and fears: Address concerns and fears that employees may have about the change. This may involve providing reassurance about job security, addressing concerns about new technologies, or providing additional training and support to help employees feel more comfortable with the change.

Provide clear guidance: Provide clear guidance on what is expected of employees in the new data culture. This can help reduce uncertainty and make the change feel more manageable.

Celebrate successes: Celebrate successes along the way and recognize employees who are contributing to the change process. This can help build momentum and increase employee buy-in.

Lead by example: Leaders must lead by example and model the desired behaviours and practices. This can involve changing leadership styles, communication methods, and decision-making processes.

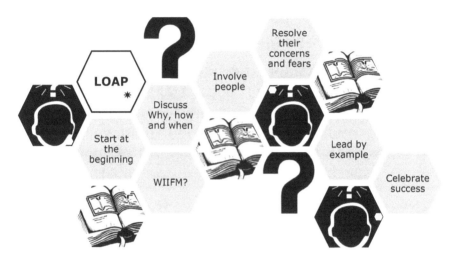

LOAP - Learning on a Page 7 - Strategies for overcoming resistance to change.

And keep in mind:

"Nothing great was ever achieved without enthusiasm." (Ralph Waldo Emerson)

In Berry's case, her light bulb moment was matching together the what's in it for me question, with a focus on the majority of where the organisations people (the 70) were, and identifying those stakeholders who were motivated to improve resource deployment efficiency and effectiveness, as we'll see a bit later.

Data governance and data culture

To build a data culture, it is important to establish data governance policies and procedures to ensure that data is managed effectively and efficiently. This includes defining who has access to data, how it is stored, and how it is used.

Here are some key data governance practices that you can consider to build your data culture:

Data privacy and security: Establish policies and procedures to protect sensitive and confidential data from unauthorized access, use, disclosure, or destruction.

Data quality management: Implement procedures to ensure that data is accurate, consistent, and reliable. This includes defining data standards, establishing data validation rules, and conducting regular data quality checks.

Data access and sharing: Define who has access to data and how it can be shared. This includes establishing access controls and permissions, as well as procedures for sharing data with internal and external stakeholders.

Data retention and archiving: Define data retention policies to ensure that data is retained for the appropriate amount of time and is securely archived when it is no longer needed.

Data integration and interoperability: Establish policies and procedures to ensure that data can be integrated and exchanged between different systems and applications.

Data ownership and accountability: Define roles and responsibilities for managing data and assign ownership to different data sets to ensure accountability.

Data governance structure: Establish a data governance structure that defines the roles and responsibilities of different stakeholders involved in managing data.

We've already talked about the importance of having and understanding people's roles and responsibilities. It's really important to establish and embed this in your data governance model too. For example, who or what are the data owners, the data stewards?

Data Owner A person who is:	• generally in a senior position, responsible for the categorization, protection, usage, and quality of one or more data sets.
Data Steward A person who is:	• in an oversight or data governance role, responsible for ensuring the quality and fitness for purpose of the organization's data assets, including the metadata for those data assets.

These are just examples. Use them, change, add to them as you determine fit for your purpose, organisation and your culture.

Invest in a data Infrastructure.

For a data culture to grow and develop you need to provide the organisation and its people with the tools to use data to drive decision making within the business. This means investing in the technology and infrastructure to make this possible

A robust data infrastructure can promote a data culture by:

Making the data accessible: A robust data infrastructure enables employees to easily access data from various sources, such as databases, data warehouses, and data lakes. When data is easily accessible, employees are more likely to use it in their daily work and decision-making processes.

Improving data quality: "Rubbish in Rubbish out" Investing in a data infrastructure can also improve the quality of data by ensuring that it is accurate, consistent, and up to date. When employees can rely on the data they are working with, they are more likely to use it in their decision-making processes.

Providing tools for data analysis: Allowing employees to turn that raw data into meaningful actionable information. A data infrastructure can provide tools and resources for employees to analyse and visualize data, such as dashboards, reports, and analytics platforms. When employees have access to these tools, they can more easily interpret and understand the data, leading to more informed decision-making.

Promoting collaboration across the business: A data infrastructure can also facilitate collaboration between employees by enabling them to share data and insights with each other. This can help create a culture of data-driven decision-making by encouraging employees to use data to support their ideas and proposals.

Ensure that the organisation has the necessary technology and infrastructure to collect, store, and analyse data. This may include investing in data analytics tools, data storage solutions, and other infrastructure that can help the organisation use data effectively.

Self-service analysis

With the infrastructure in place it is important to make data available to staff who can use that data to inform their actions, so enabling self-service is important. This can bring challenges in its own right "*It's not how things are done around here*" can rear its head at this point but you should persevere. Remember a primary aim of investment in the data infrastructure is to enable the self-serve ability of your organisations people.

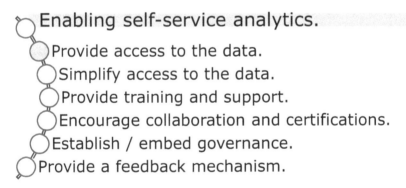

Enabling self-service analytics.

Provide access to the data.

Simplify access to the data.

Provide training and support.

Encourage collaboration and certifications.

Establish / embed governance.

Provide a feedback mechanism.

Figure 21 - Enabling self-service analytics.

Enabling self-service analytics is an important part of building a data-driven culture and empowering users to make data-driven decisions. If and how you provide self-service analysis capability will depend on your business. Listed here are some ways you can enable self-service analytics so users can explore data and generate insights independently:

Provide access to data: Ensure that users have access to the data they need to perform self-service analytics. This may involve providing access to data warehouses, data lakes, or other data sources.

Simplify data access: Make it easy for users to access and query data, even if they don't have specialised data skills. This can involve using tools like Power BI to create intuitive dashboards and reports that allow users to interact with data in a user-friendly way.

Provide training and support: Provide training and support to help users build the skills they need to perform self-service analytics. This may involve offering training on data analysis tools, such as Power BI or Excel, or providing access to online training resources.

Encourage collaboration: Encourage collaboration and knowledge sharing among users. This can help users learn from one another and build a sense of community around data analytics.

Implement data governance: Implement data governance policies and procedures to ensure that users are working with accurate, complete, and consistent data. This can involve establishing data quality standards, defining data ownership and accountability, and setting up data security and privacy protocols.

Provide user feedback mechanisms: Provide user feedback mechanisms to capture user feedback and suggestions for improvement. This can help ensure that users feel heard and valued, and that the self-service analytics tools are meeting their needs.

Overall, enabling self-service analytics requires a combination of technical tools, training, and governance. By providing access to data, simplifying data access, providing training and support, encouraging collaboration, implementing data governance, and providing user feedback mechanisms, you can empower users to explore data and generate insights independently.

Invest in people.

What is the point undertaking all this effort if you don't invest in your people? Your people are central to becoming a data driven culture organisation. We hope we've made this absolutely clear already. Even in the modern AI world, for the majority of us it's still humans who are making the decisions, hopefully based on the data. As you'll see in the next section; Change is hard if you don't invest in skills. People will become anxious. And that will not help. So you should:

Provide training: Provide employees with training and development opportunities to help them become more data literate.

This can include data analysis and visualisation tools, training on data management, and other relevant training that will help employees become more comfortable with using data to make decisions.

Training is not just for the data team though. It's perhaps as, if not more, important to encourage knowledge gain with users and senior leadership teams too. As we've noted, Gartner have indicated that Data Literacy is the number 2 roadblock for CDO's.

As an example, they may not need Power BI training, but if you're using a certain survey method or statistical analysis technique, you need to make sure that your stakeholders do understand what the data is telling them. Understanding the implications, benefits, risks, constraints of one data capture / survey method over another or one visualisation technique over another, we believe is pretty important. After all, "*if you assume, you make an ass out of you and me*".

Encourage experimentation: Encourage employees to experiment with data and to use it to test new ideas and approaches. This can help to build a culture of innovation and encourage employees to use data to drive growth and improve outcomes.

That doesn't have to translate into a large investment of money, time and people. We discussed earlier a financial services organisation's people development forum initiative. Could you do similar? If you started small, isn't it easier to find the time, people and perhaps a small sum of money to invest? It also gives you something to act with, some evidence of progress and some buy in and confidence?

What sort of people do you need?

As an alternative way of considering this to the discussions we've already had around roles, responsibilities, skills etc.

Think about people as being a big part of your organisation's data ecosystem.

Lots of organisations either have or are going down the route of distributed decision making with decentralised, empowered people. These people are on the front lines, adapting to changes without, or with only quite limited, central command and control approvals. Great!

The organisation itself though still needs to function. Without it, overall customers aren't served, employees aren't paid. So, its divisions and departments, the people within, need to engage, talk and interact with each other as seamlessly as possible. If not, things are likely to slow down, grind to a halt and potentially cease to exist.

So at the very least each department needs people, with the right skills, who understand their roles and responsibilities. They need data, information, to execute processes and deliver to their responsibilities. They hand this data off and get it back from other departments and people. So data is flowing around your organisation, interacting with your people, all the time. Like it or not!

Now whatever their motivation, those people don't set out every morning to do a bad job do they? There are various academic and practical studies and papers available to perhaps understand what people want from their work. By all means google them. Whether that's financial rewards, security, and work life balance, we're not intending to explore. But the data itself doesn't desire financial recompense, security or balance, does it? It's ambivalent to these.

If you'd allow us to offer a touch of humour. Data though is a force of nature! It gets everywhere. So how might you assemble the right team?

For a bit of fun with insight. Adding to the previous example ubiquitous RACI model, here's our own adaption. Data driven team behaviours:

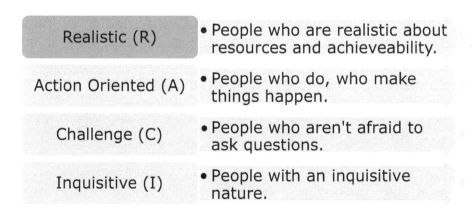

Realistic (R)	• People who are realistic about resources and achieveability.
Action Oriented (A)	• People who do, who make things happen.
Challenge (C)	• People who aren't afraid to ask questions.
Inquisitive (I)	• People with an inquisitive nature.

Figure 22 - Data driven team behaviours?

OK it's a bit corny. However it does fit with many of our key messages and TNT's such as:

- Under promise, over deliver.
- Objections are buying signals.
- Start with the end in mind.
- Practice what you preach.
- Find the golden thread.
- Ask the same question in different ways.

Before we move on to the next section as we're having fun, here's a quick riddle:

Question: "*What can fill a room but takes up no space*"?

Answer: "*Light*"!

And that, we honestly consider is what you're seeking with the people you want. You want those that can help shed some light on things, don't you? And once you've seen the light, you want people who can get on and do things and meet the expectations that have perhaps been set. So you do want people who are:

- Inquisitive.
- Challenge minded.
- Action Oriented.
- Realistic.

As a final comment on investing in your people:

You've found the people you want. They have a great balance of soft skills and technical expertise. They can help you seek out the light. You hire them.

Why then haven't you thought through what they are going to do from the off? Come on, you know it's true!

Frankly our own experience has been that we've been delighted that someone has actually thought to provide a desk or place an order for a laptop, let alone work out what they want us to do, aside from carry out all the mandatory computer based training modules we need!

Seriously though, why is our natural tendency to "ease people in"? It may be that you don't want them to fail. Fair enough. It may be that you want them to prove themselves before giving them something which is hard to do, or perhaps what they really should be doing. OK we get that too.

But this is about being a data driven culture. It's about focusing on different thinking to that already within BAU? It's about embracing and driving change. It's about delivering the future, isn't it?

So why not ask a question at the interview along the lines of:

> Tell us how you prepared for this chat, the thinking you went through, the approach you took, the things you considered but discarded and why.

These may give you an alternative insight to a typical question such as,

> Tell us about a time when you had to engage in a difficult situation and get a tricky stakeholder on board.

Don't misunderstand us, we're not saying a competency based question similar to that is bad. We are saying, that if you ask the same sort of question in a different way, you are gathering more data. You may get a different answer or a similar one. Either way you could well be on the right track to knowing if the person is right or not. If they ask you good questions, happy days! They are trying to gather data too.

If you break it down, in this case all you are really doing is perhaps gaining further insight into their CV claims that they are great communicators, have fantastic stakeholder management skills, are highly inquisitive etc. Surely, it's better to seek actual evidence not theoretical or possibly even made up?

These inquisitive thinkers, communication savvy, proactive action oriented skills are the very ones that research says are most missing. They are the very ones you want, aren't they?

So why haven't you lined up some good engagement, investigative based opportunities, not technical production ones, that would be a good way to see how they go about that task, before they start? You have to be prepared to spend time working with and alongside them.

Your situation may be different, after all, all organisations are. However the research is clear. People with the softer skills are in demand, and always have been. Because people make the world go around, they make things happen.

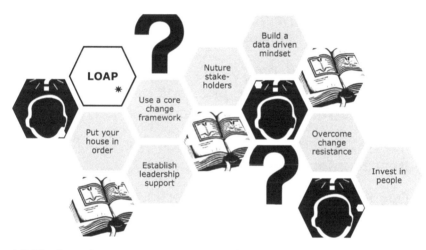

LOAP - Learning on a Page 8 - A step by step guide to building a data driven culture.

CHANGE IS HARD.

Despite what we have said so far, Cultural change is hard. And we know building a data culture is cultural change for an organisation. But:

"Without ambition one starts nothing. Without work one finishes nothing. The prize will not be sent to you. You have to win it." (Ralph Waldo Emerson)

Difficulties can arise for several reasons which we have addressed in previous sections:

- Deeply ingrained culture / Inertia. If you're working for a business that has sold insurance in the City of London very successfully for 250 years and is still selling insurance successfully today and hasn't adopted a data-driven culture, what's your incentive to change? Why bother? You might get *"This is how we do things around here"* if you're lucky enough to actually get a response!

- Resistance to change. If you don't know what the vision is or can't understand what's in it for you, again, what's your incentive to change?

- Lack of leadership desire. The clue is in the title, leaders are supposed to lead, aren't they? Have a look at some of our "Do's and Don'ts" later for some guidance.

- Complexity of change: Cultural change can be complex and multifaceted, requiring changes in attitudes, behaviours, communication, processes, and leadership. It can also require coordinated efforts from multiple stakeholders, making it challenging to achieve.

Learning how to use the new software and even the new processes that the software might prescribe can, often be the easiest part to achieve. Dealing with the people behaviours and ways of working, howsoever ingrained they may be, is the hard part.

And that's one reason why we like our full amended version of Lippitt-Knoster's core framework for change.

Vision	Agreement	Skills	Benefits	Resources	Culture	Action		Outcomes
✓	✓	✓	✓	✓	✓	✓	→	Success
✗	✓	✓	✓	✓	✓	✓	→	Confusion
✓	✗	✓	✓	✓	✓	✓	→	Sabotage
✓	✓	✗	✓	✓	✓	✓	→	Anxiety
✓	✓	✓	✗	✓	✓	✓	→	Resistance
✓	✓	✓	✓	✗	✓	✓	→	Frustration
✓	✓	✓	✓	✓	✗	✓	→	Dissent
✓	✓	✓	✓	✓	✓	✗	→	Treadmill

Figure 23 - Our amended Lippitt-Knoster core framework for change.

To us, there's a heavy explicit and implicit focus on people. Hopefully you see that too?

If you intend to make your data driven journey a success, you need to address all of these. Failing to manage even one, can lead to failure!

Vision

We've already discussed the need for the Vision to be clear, compelling and directly related to solving the problems that exist. Start with Why is our number 1 key message.

Without Vision, people are confused.

What should you watch out for? If people are saying "how should I / do you expect me to do this?", it's another way of saying "why should I do it?" Use our PR model to help you see things through their lens.

"Life is a journey, not a destination." (Ralph Waldo Emerson)

Agreement / consensus

We think it's largely a given that in most organisations today, the underlying concept of buy-in is critical. Without agreement, consensus, you risk explicit or implicit sabotage.

An Army general once said: *"No plan survives contact with the enemy."* Similarly no strategic plan survives contact with the marketplace, which would include your internal stakeholders and users. Be prepared to change the plan in the light of new circumstances and the unforeseen.

Skills

Do you have the know-how to do this? If a skill and/training is lacking, at best people will be anxious. At worst outright failure beckons. We discussed this right from the outset.

> What skills are needed?

> How will you get those that you don't sufficiently have?

> How will people be trained?

> Have you done a skills assessment?

Have a look at the roles you might need, what skills typically might these roles bring? Have you identified all the required data roles and responsibilities, did any skill gaps come up?

Benefits / incentives

Are you doing the right things? Do people see the benefits? Can they be achieved? How will it benefit us the people? No-one likes the feeling of things being a waste of time. Resistance is the natural outcome for a lack of buy in here.

Don't forget there are two sides to this. There are the benefits to the organisation. Generally, if done correctly, these are perhaps easier to get one's head around, however they can be a tad abstract sometimes, with people saying, *"I get that, but it's doesn't apply to me"*.

There are also the benefits, or perhaps you prefer, incentives, to the actual people. You might see it all, and you might enjoy changing, you're at the heart of it! But if you don't keep your key stakeholders engaged, focus on what's in it for them, at the very least it will take time. It may well be resisted! People will simply try to stick to the old ways of working, that they know-how to do.

Resources

How often might you have heard:

> "They want us to do more with less" or

> "How will I get enough support?"

> "Will there be time to gain the experience once we've been trained to bed things in?"

> "We haven't got the budget for that."

People get really frustrated when then don't feel like they are getting enough of the right support to get the job done. Which can lead to , *"why should I bother"*? or *"I'll just do the minimum required of me"*.

If you set your stall out too early with what you can do and what you want, it's really hard to backtrack and get what you then need!

Culture

There's a theme in this book of "*That's not the way we do things around here*". And as we know, "*Culture eats strategy for breakfast*"! On the soccer field, players can get booked (usually a yellow card) for dissent. They act or say something to show how they disagree, they dissent! Now they might eventually "comply" with the decision, but you can bet they aren't happy!

It's similar with your people. If they don't agree with something, or don't want to do it, how often is it that that thing is done right first time and quickly? Not very? So in effect, they dissent! And at best things don't get done very well or quickly.

Actions

"*The most important advice I give to young people is … just learn how to get stuff done.*" (Barack Obama)

If you don't actually do anything, nothing will get done. Preferably, things will be done to a plan, that's been jointly developed by a skilled and experienced representative group. Without it, people may feel as if they are running but not moving forwards, just like being on a treadmill.

Keep your project on a page.

If you can't summarize your project vision on a page, then you run the risk of lacking clarity. If you lack clarity, then you may struggle to build consensus.

Many of the most successful programmes and projects begin with a very high-level visualisation of what they are trying to achieve. A mind-map, or a one-page diagram, can be a really helpful way to summarise or visualise your goals and the journey required to reach them.

Consider creating an image like this to support your communications and description of the vision at the outset. It's a very practical tip, but it can pay dividends.

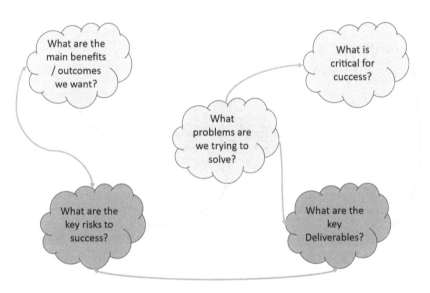

Figure 24 - Keep your project on a page.

Don't forget "more haste, less speed" too. Setting off in the wrong direction, too early, perhaps with insufficient skill or resource can be just as unproductive as taking no actions.

"*Come on Art, just do it*, do some actions".

Don't stop here!

Have you ever been involved in a business change project that didn't value user adoption as a key outcome? No? Nor have we!

So why do we all stop shortly after go-live? You want to establish a data driven culture for business reasons don't you. Establishing a data driven culture is arguably one of THE business change initiatives your organisation will ever undertake? It is a marathon not a sprint. You must be committed for the long game. Your change is likely to have 3 states. Current, transition and future. Doing 2 out of 3 is bad!

Figure 25 - Why do we all stop here?

More on know-how and Skills

We thought we'd start our path to the summary by providing some *"real life"* examples, for an attempt at a bit of fun. If you don't enjoy what you do, why bother! Firstly:

The parable of the engineer and the hammer:

"A factory owner hired an engineer to fix a broken-down engine. The engineer inspected the engine for one minute, took out his hammer, hammered the engine once, and then started the engine with no problem.

The engineer charged the factory owner $5000. The factory owner was shocked, protested that the engineer had worked for only one minute, and asked for an itemized bill. The engineer sent the factory owner an itemized bill:

Hammering the engine: $5

Knowing where to hammer the engine: $4,995".

Skills are for using.

The following image is taken from a linked post of someone who runs and executive search consultancy specialising in data and analytics. Someone who likely knows first-hand the frustrations of an organisation paying lip service to data. Imagine having a CDO but they are not on the c-suite and not really front of mind. They don't report to the CEO.

This is what ambitious Data Leaders think:

"How do I get my CEO to give a shit about what I do If I don't report to them".

Now, let's quantify what we mean by "Give a Shit", because all CEO's will claim they give a shit about what all of the senior Execs in the business are doing.

But if they really 'gave a shit' about Data, then the Data Leader would always be in the room every time there is a strategic conversation about the business.

If they really gave a shit a Data Strategy would be crucial to the major pivot in business strategy that the company is taking.

So back to the Question – "How do you get the CEO to give a shit".

No easy answers here, as in many cases it won't be possible.

It's an age demographic thing.

This CEO has 5 years left max; and it's probably going to be 10 years until the tide goes out and the world realises the company are screwed because they never placed Data in a strategic position in the business.

By that stage the CEO and rest of the C-Suite is long gone, feet up, retired. So they don't care.

The Data Leader can either just move on to business who get's it, which is not easy. Or they can wait around for the C-Suite lead to change and hope for a better seat at the table.

#datastrategy #dataleadership #dataanalytics

Changing an organisation's culture requires a sustained effort to overcome these challenges and create a new culture that reflects new values, beliefs, and practices. It may require a significant investment of time, resources, and leadership commitment to achieve cultural change successfully.

Taking a liberty with this great quote.

"*It doesn't make sense to hire smart people and then ~~tell them what to do~~ ignore them; we hire smart people so they can tell us what to do.*" – (Steve Jobs)

Just do it.

"Just do it", create a data culture. Take some advice from Art Williams. You have to start; you have to keep going. Just do it, until the job gets done.

For those that don't know who Art Williams is, let us give a little background on Art and why perhaps what he says is relevant to those on this organisational data journey. The internet and Wikipedia have this to say about Art:

Art Williams is an American entrepreneur and motivational speaker who is best known for founding the insurance company, A.L. Williams & Associates, which later became Primerica Financial Services. Williams was born in 1942 in Cairo, Georgia, and grew up in a poor family, where he learned the value of hard work and determination.

Williams started his career as a high school football coach and later worked as a state football championship referee. In the 1970s, he began selling insurance part-time, and in 1977, he founded A.L. Williams & Associates with a mission to provide affordable life insurance to middle-class families.

Williams' company grew rapidly, and he became a millionaire in a short time. He was known for his charismatic leadership style and his motivational speeches, which he delivered to his salesforce. In 1987, Williams gave a speech to his salesforce titled "Just Do It," which became one of his most famous speeches.

The "Just Do It" speech was inspired by Williams' experience as a football coach, where he learned the importance of taking action and not letting fear hold you back. He encouraged his salesforce to adopt a similar mentality and to take action without fear of failure.

The speech became a rallying cry for his salesforce, who went on to achieve great success under Williams' leadership. The success of A.L. Williams & Associates attracted the attention of Wall Street, and in 1989, the company went public.

Today, Art Williams is retired from the insurance business, but he continues to be a sought-after motivational speaker, delivering speeches on leadership, entrepreneurship, and personal development. His "Just Do It" speech has become a classic in the field of motivational speaking and is still studied and emulated by speakers and leaders today.

One of our favourite quotes from his speech is this, it makes us want to start doing, not talking about it, not about why it's a good idea to build a data culture but to actually start. Remember this is taken from a speech written in the 1980s and its about succeeding at business. Really, it's about building an effective organisational culture and encouraging people to take action.

"I think it's almost impossible for a smart person to win in business in America today, because I find smart people spend their whole lifetime figuring things out. They always trying to figure out an easier way, and a quicker way. And another thing I found out about smart people; is they just don't get around to doing nothing." (Art Williams)

So taking a lead from Art Williams here. How do you build a data culture in your organisation today? Whether it's large or small, in the public or private sector, Art says:

- o *"You just do it".*

- o *"You got to be tough, and you can't quit".*

- o *"You got to be a leader".*

- o *"You do whatever it takes to get the job done".*

- o *"What's the primary difference between winners and losers?*

"The winners do it, and do it, and do it, and do it....until the job gets done".

Remember, building a data culture can have a significant positive impact on your business. If you're on that journey or thinking about starting, just do it, keep going, don't quit. Just do it.

Do's and don'ts.

In our experience, here's a few examples of what a CDO **should** and **should not** be doing as part of the programme. Remember it's people, process, data and technology. In that order, for a reason.

This quote now hopefully correctly stated is so good we've used it twice.

"It doesn't make sense to hire smart people and then tell them what to do; we hire smart people so they can tell us what to do." (Steve Jobs)

What a CDO should do:	What a CDO Shouldn't do:
Establish Direction	Take a back seat
Align People	Usurp the team
Develop the vision, strategy, roadmap	Dictate directions
Engage Stakeholders	Ignore / Don't Listen
Manage Expectations	Be principal / only requirements giver
Walk the walk	Dictate the answer
Be a powerful advocate	
Obtain and allocate the Skills and Resources	
Encourage inquisitiveness	
Keep the big picture vision, purpose in mind	
Monitor and actively manage risk	
Ensure contingency, manage costs	
Focus on Outcomes	

Figure 26 - Do's and Don'ts

What should you do if your data is wrong?

There's only one way to say this - BE CAREFUL!

No-one likes to be told their stuff is rubbish or they've been doing it wrong all this time. At best it just shows them in a (very) bad light. Not the way to win hearts and minds.

In one Digital Processing Outsourcer, whilst they had "proper" finance systems, these systems generally showed information at a summary level and didn't have "revenue recognition" details.

For clarity, recognised revenue is typically what accountants permit to be stated in financial statements. Say as a simple example you sold annual support and maintenance service polices, paid annually. Simplifying one might essentially divide the annual amount by 12 and then "recognise" $1/12^{th}$ of that annual sum as the months rolled by.

In this case, client chargeable IT services was the recognised revenue. This data was held on a spreadsheet. Sound familiar? Monthly, an IT mid-level manager would manually review timesheets, which were also a bit of a lottery, for accuracy and timeliness. The manager would subjectively estimate the % of the job then complete. It wasn't a total guess, the manager had experience, did do some investigative digging and did use their judgement. But nevertheless it was not uncommon for these estimates to simply be wrong, by enough. There were typically between 150 and 200 jobs / projects in flight to manually consider every month. They did their best.

Essentially, these figures were just entered into the proper systems to produce the relevant financial statements, effectively on trust. The mid-level manager was not party to how and why this information was used by the leaders.

Said outsourcer was backed / funded by Venture Capitalists and was about to seek further funding.

The outsourcer's problem was that some of their clients' expectations weren't being satisfactorily met by the IT services work being done. These clients stated that weren't going to pay any more until their initial expectations had been met. So the Outsourcer had to swallow the extra IT development and fix costs and absorb the re-work.

The IT Exec stakeholder changed and started to try and understand what they had inherited. In summary this equated to a lot of unpaid re-work. They knew financial statements would influence the funding process. If they re-stated the %'s complete, this would show the job wasn't as complete as stated and the recognised revenue to date was therefore wrong.

Restating financial statements, particularly well after the event, is not something to do lightly. Particularly if funding might be influenced.

We can't possibly say if this was true or fictitious. If even some of it was true, many of our techniques noted herein might have come into play. Manage expectations; Under promise, over deliver; Measure twice, cut once, and so on.

Just be careful, IF your data is wrong!

WHAT'S POWER BI GOT TO DO WITH THIS ANYWAY?

Let's revisit what makes building a data culture difficult and let's revisit some of the challenges that Berry is facing:

o Lack of executive support

o Resistance to change.

o Siloed data

o Data quality issues

o Lack of data literacy

o Security and privacy concerns

It's likely that Berry will need to address most if not all of those things although some might be more important than others. Remember "timing is everything".

One of the subtle but very important keys to building a data driven culture, is telling the data driven to story to the right people, in the right place at the right time. Taking liberties with the famous Martini advert, here's our *"Martini data storytelling"* key message:

Key Message

Tell the right data story, to the right people, in the right rlace, at the right time

Key Message 25 - Right data story, right people, right place, right time.

You could also add "*in the right way*" too.

If you don't tell the right story, to the right people, in the right place and the right time, and nobody acts on the data or analysis you have done then it's pretty much wasted effort. For clarity, that doesn't mean the data will show a change is needed or that judgements will always be to change. Do nothing, just say no, are all valid actions too.

HOW CAN POWER BI HELP YOU?

Power BI can help solve some of the data culture difficulties businesses and CDOs face. Other tools and technologies can assist here too, but we have grown up with Microsoft data technologies and Power BI. So, for us anyway, Power BI can play a key role. Just remember that if your organisation doesn't have Power BI, refuses to use MSFT technology or has another platform there other tools that can help in these areas too.

We've already said that in today's modern organisation there's already a lot of technology available to help, perhaps without having to invest in anything new. If you haven't got Power BI (or similar), you probably have Excel (or its equivalent)? Yes, it might not be the best tool to run your organisation on. However you've got it, it's already paid for, so why not use it, to begin with. You also probably know enough about how to use it too. So the learning curve isn't too high.

If you're using SQL Server database on premise, then your IT team are probably familiar with SQL Server, Reporting Services (SSRS), Analysis Services (SSAS), Integration Services (SSIS). Whilst individually or collectively perhaps not as holistic as Power BI, nevertheless they exist already and could play a part.

With Microsoft "Office", you may also have other things like Content search, E-Discovery, Compliance centre, Purview? This is inevitably going to depend on your type of Microsoft 365 / Office 365 licence. This isn't intended as an exhaustive list, it's just to get you thinking about what you may already have access to. It's also quite likely, isn't it, that our friends at Microsoft will add more capabilities, tools and maybe even change the names of them (surely not!).

Even if you don't have a Power BI tenant, you can currently download Power BI desktop (Power BI authoring tool) for free. There are limitations, like lack of collaboration, security and integration but if you're a smaller business, this could be a way of starting cheaply for you.

Power BI can be used right across the organisation. Or perhaps to qualify that a little, in our experience at least across the "business" side of an organisation. It could be in, with, across, Marketing, Sales, Operations, Procurement, Legal, Finance and Banking, HR etc.

It is probably better to focus on things that aren't already being done with sufficient insight. ***If it isn't broken, don't fix it***.

Many organisations do desire enough data, to help them understand, measure, engage, improve and even retire their products, solutions and services. They want to work out if and how to improve things like engagement, utilisation, finances, service, effectiveness, efficiency etc. They want insight into the value that they provide to their customers and stakeholders.

Remember that every situation is different. You may have other ideas and challenges. That's for you to discover. We're just trying to give you some ideas.

That said, we're definitely not saying that data monitoring, capture, extraction, transformation, analysis etc. are new.

There are many industries and sectors where technologies have existed for decades to help with such data driven insight. Good examples might include "heavy / engineering" industries. Just as one small example, consider Telemetry / Scada.

SCADA is Supervisory Control and Data Acquisition (Telemetry) and is used for controlling, monitoring, and analyzing industrial devices and processes. Aside from being well established there is often the need for "ruggedized" solutions herein, which do cost money.

Mind you, your SCADA or Telemetry system could perhaps be a data source for combining with other data sources in Power BI.

So let's start by summarising our view of what Power BI is pretty good at.

What's Power BI pretty good at?

Keeping this simple, as we suspect otherwise, we'll have to update it very frequently to keep up with its development. Power BI is, in our opinion, good at

- Connecting to lots of data sources quickly, to find the data you're seeking.

- Building unified data models from these sources.

- Enhance that data adding more context or further data.

- Creating compelling visuals and dashboards

- Helping to tell the stories in the right place e.g. embedding into your Phone, Teams, SharePoint, PowerPoint apps or getting a feed of information right into your mailbox by subscription.

To repeat a couple of key messages, this is about Martini data storytelling and it's about your audience. It doesn't have to be Hi-tech either.

We probably all know that there's an awful lot of data analysis in professional sport? Take football (soccer) as an example. Lots of different data is captured. Player's pitch movement and locations; how far they run; how many tackles, assists, goals and so on. No doubt those involved in the monitoring and detailed analysis are probably pretty technically skilled. But not everyone necessarily is.

Even if the manager / coach is technology savvy that doesn't mean that they do want to pour over a spreadsheet or a digital dashboard to get the insight they are looking for. They do want to decide who should be selected for the next game and how the team should change their approach. That's where they add their value. So they want to work in the way best suited to them!

As an example, we're reliably told that some managers simply prefer to have a printed piece of paper, containing the agreed level of analysis (and recommendations perhaps) placed on their desk, first thing in the morning whilst they may be having their first cup of coffee. That's fine, if that's the way they want to see the data, that's their call.

You get our point?

So, if these are of value to you, Power BI can help:

Fixing siloed data

Power BI can help remove the silo data problem by enabling users to access and analyse data from multiple sources in a centralized and consistent manner. Power BI can be an end to end analytical solution, and as such has features that can help you work with data from across your technology estate.

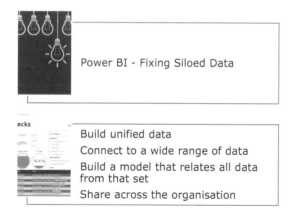

Figure 27 - Power BI – Fixing siloed data.

Here are some ways in which Power BI can help remove data silos:

Data connectivity: Power BI supports connectivity to a wide range of data sources, including cloud-based and on-premises data sources. This allows users to access data from multiple sources in a centralized and consistent manner, without the need for manual data transfers or redundant data storage.

Data modelling: Power BI allows users to create data models that consolidate and unify data from multiple sources, providing a consistent view of the data across the organisation. This can help remove data silos by enabling users to access and analyse data in a standardized and consistent manner.

Collaboration and sharing: Power BI allows users to collaborate and share reports and dashboards with other users in the organisation, enabling knowledge sharing and cross-functional collaboration. This can help remove data silos by providing users with access to data from other departments and business units.

Data quality issues

Power BI can help fix data quality issues by providing a range of tools and features that enable users to monitor, clean, and improve data quality.

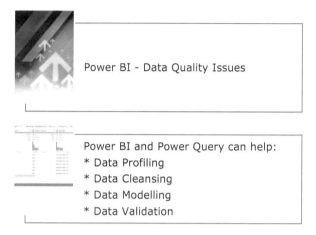

Power BI - Data Quality Issues

Power BI and Power Query can help:
* Data Profiling
* Data Cleansing
* Data Modelling
* Data Validation

Figure 28 - Power BI - Fixing data quality issues.

Here are some ways in which Power BI can help fix data quality issues:

Data profiling: Power BI allows users to profile their data, which involves analysing the data to identify any quality issues or anomalies. This can help users gain a better understanding of their data and identify areas where data quality can be improved.

Data cleansing: Power BI allows users to clean their data, which involves identifying and correcting any errors or inconsistencies in the data. This can include removing duplicates, correcting spelling errors, and standardizing data formats.

Data modelling: Power BI allows users to create data models that consolidate and unify data from multiple sources, providing a consistent view of the data across the organisation. This can help improve data quality by

199

enabling users to identify and correct inconsistencies in the data.

Data validation: Power BI allows users to validate their data, which involves ensuring that the data conforms to a set of predefined rules or standards. This can help improve data quality by ensuring that the data is accurate, complete, and consistent.

Data governance: Power BI supports data governance, which enables administrators to control access to data and ensure compliance with data security policies. This can help improve data quality by providing a centralized and secure approach to data management.

Earlier we suggested that Berry could think about some of the DAMA guidelines and work out if her force's data was accurate, current, secure and valid. Overall, Power BI can help fix these and other data quality issues by providing users with powerful tools and features for data profiling, data cleansing, data modelling, data validation, and data governance. By leveraging these capabilities, organisations can improve the accuracy, completeness, and consistency of their data, enabling better decision-making and more successful outcomes.

And whilst data quality may not be the easiest sell internally, if this work was done, perhaps even just as a proof of concept, could this inform levels of resistance to change, what literacy does exist and what pace of change might be achieved with the right resources?

Improving data literacy

How can Power BI help improve data literacy:

Data visualisation: Power BI allows users to create interactive and visually appealing data visualisations, which can help users better understand and interpret complex data. This can help promote data literacy by providing users with more accessible and user-friendly data insights.

Self-service analytics: Power BI supports self-service analytics, which enables users to explore and analyse data on their own, without requiring assistance from IT or data analysts. This can help promote data literacy by empowering users to access and analyse data independently.

Training and resources: Power BI provides a range of training and resources, including online courses, tutorials, and documentation, that can help users develop their data literacy skills. These resources can help users learn how to use Power BI effectively, as well as develop their data analysis and visualisation skills.

Collaboration and sharing: Power BI allows users to collaborate and share reports and dashboards with other users in the organisation, enabling knowledge sharing and cross-functional collaboration. This can help promote data literacy by providing users with access to data from other departments and business units.

Data governance: Power BI supports data governance, which enables administrators to control access to data and ensure compliance with data security policies. This can help promote data literacy by providing a centralized and secure approach to data management, which can help users develop a better understanding of data privacy and security.

Dealing with security, privacy and governance concerns

Power BI provides several features and capabilities that can address security and privacy concerns.

Power BI security and privacy
- Role based security
- Row level security
- Encryption
- Compliance and certifications
- Microsoft Purview and Information Protection

Figure 29 - Power BI dealing with security and privacy concerns.

Here are some ways in which Power BI can address security and privacy concerns:

Role-based security: Power BI allows administrators to define role-based security, which involves assigning users to different roles and granting access to reports and dashboards based on those roles. This can help ensure that users only have access to the data that is relevant to their job function.

Row-level security: Power BI allows administrators to implement row-level security, which involves restricting access to specific rows of data based on user roles or criteria. This can help ensure that sensitive data is only accessible to authorized users.

Encryption: Power BI supports encryption of data at rest and in transit, which can help protect data from unauthorized access or disclosure. This can help ensure that data is kept confidential and secure.

Compliance and certifications: Power BI is compliant with a range of industry and regulatory standards, such as ISO 27001 and GDPR, and has obtained certifications from third-party auditors, such as SOC 2 and HIPAA. This can help ensure that data is managed and stored in a secure and compliant manner.

Microsoft Information Protection (MIP) is a cloud-based service provided by Microsoft that helps organisations protect sensitive data across different platforms and applications, including Power BI. MIP provides a range of security and privacy features and capabilities, including:

Classification: MIP allows organisations to classify their data based on its sensitivity, importance, and other criteria. This can help organisations identify and protect sensitive data and ensure that it is only accessible to authorized users.

Labelling: MIP allows organisations to apply labels to their data, which can include information such as sensitivity, confidentiality, and retention policies. This can help ensure that data is managed and stored in a compliant and secure manner.

Protection: MIP provides protection capabilities that can help prevent data leakage or unauthorized access to sensitive data. This can include encryption of data at rest and in transit, as well as access controls and data loss prevention (DLP) policies.

Monitoring and reporting: MIP provides monitoring and reporting capabilities that can help organisations track and report on data usage and security incidents. This can help organisations identify and respond to potential security threats or data breaches.

Examples of data driven insight

We thought, keeping it simple, we'd offer, a few examples across customer, operational and technical areas, just to get you thinking and a few tips to be wary of too.

The truth is out there.

Customer engagement / retention.
For B2C organisations, many of their customers simply don't truly interact with them much or regularly once they've bought whatever product or paid to receive the service. Often because they have no need to do so. The customers have what they wanted in the first place, nothing has gone wrong, they are not interested in anything else as yet, they haven't needed to update any of their details and so on.

So how does the organisation know if their customers are truly engaged, happy, supportive, loyal and likely to renew or recommend them to someone else?

There may be loyalty schemes, net promoter scores and other customer surveys.

> But how accurate are these?

> How many people proportionate to the overall customer or service user base does it represent?

> How often or recently has the data been collected?

> Can any of it be relied upon?

> How many housing tenants regularly interact, and on what matter?

> How many council taxpayers complain about the state of the roads?

> How many parents state they are happy with their child's education?

> How many library users are there, how often do they visit?

> What areas, districts do these people live in?

> How many customers, of what segment, in which area, are likely to commit fraud?

All proportionate to the customer base size.

We're not trying to be controversial or say some of this thinking and analysis isn't being done and put to good use. We are generalising a lot simply trying to get you to think.

We're pretty sure you'd agree that the answers are along the lines of contact not reliable, recent, or consistent enough. Not across enough customers, or enough combinations of factors and so on.

Lots of good work has been done on engagement so far, but there's probably a long way to go too.

What if you could easily, quickly and accurately combine multiple sources of data, present and visualise it in different ways? And then discuss it, performing what if scenarios as you go along? It may still not cover 100% of your customer or service user base. But it's highly likely to have a far wider breadth and depth of information than when sourced, viewed from just one data silo. So much more reliable than an out of date survey.

One example is of a membership organisation who thought that they retained 95% of their members. Which sounds pretty good doesn't it? And with this knowledge they planned their forthcoming strategy.

They then dug down into the data, visualised and analysed it against certain factors, using more segmentation. They actually found that in some customer segments that they had a 98% retention rate. However in other segments it was far worse than their average.

So, had they not done this they might have found the outcomes of their strategy execution to be disappointing. As it was, they could focus their efforts on different, new value products and services to target those most at risk customers whilst targeting the original strategy to those it was intended for.

Operational service / utilisation.

Where might you have multiple relationships that all have to come together to influence or form part of an overall service? Take this trade union example.

As part of their membership the union provides a range of services for the benefit of their members. Such as influencing policy, education and qualifications, training and events, promoting good / best practice, and representing the member should their employer be making a case (e.g. negligence, malpractice, misconduct and so on) against them.

The union has Customer Relationship Management System (CRM). However, whilst it might encompass a number of the above member touch points, not all of the touch point components are within the CRM and the separate systems are not integrated with each other. The cost of integration and maintaining it, is not small.

Furthermore the above may all be pretty discrete functional areas and staffed by separate groups of specialists, needing their own solution. **One size doesn't fit all, usually**.

They knew that certain employers seem to have more potential instances of a type of case within their employers, the unions members, than other employers, areas, regions. They are wondering why.

Of course they could go out and survey the members, using the unions own in house regional teams or affiliated reps. And they probably should do that, but that takes time and money. Could there be data within any of the above systems, that might spark an idea as to why one employer when seemingly similar to another, has more potential instances of certain case types?

Getting someone to amend the master systems for each to produce that data is likely to be costly and take time. Furthermore, it's generally accepted good practice to not tinker with a core operational system too often. They often have an unfortunate habit of misbehaving following a change, don't they?

But if they could capture and extract that data into a separate place, e.g. a data warehouse or data lake, they could play with (analyse) that data to their hearts content using Power BI.

In this case things pointed back to the employment policies written by the employers.

In summary, in some employers the way these polices were written directly impacted the number of potential causes for concern, i.e. potential cases. For clarity potential cases were those that needed to be considered as they were not in line with the stated policy but didn't progress to actual cases. There was nothing really amiss, but technically it had to be considered.

Solving these, by rewriting the policy to be clearer, was a win, win, win. The employee (member) wasn't prevented from working whilst under investigation, the union could clearly evidence the value they offered to their members and the employer had a workforce that were available to work. Happy days all around.

Lies, dammed lies and statistics.

We've said this step by step guide is based on practical experience. So it would be remiss of us to not quickly remind people of a couple of key things. Firstly the common phrase lies, dammed lies and statistics.

"There are three kinds of lies: Lies, damned lies, and statistics." (Mark Twain. Others attribute it to British Prime Minister Benjamin Disraeli.) Maybe neither said it.

This usually is uttered when stakeholders don't believe the data they are being presented with.

Key Message
Beware of Lies, Dammed Lies and Statistics

Key Message 26 - Beware of Lies, Dammed Lies and Statistics.

For example. Let's say you're a Professional Services firm (e.g. a Legal practice, Accountancy firm or an IT Consultancy). You already have a 75% utilisation but want to increase it to 80%.

The suggested solution might be to automate workflow based work queues with new items of work.

Timesheet data analysis would in theory show that if each trainee, paralegal, associate, solicitor, partner or in the world of IT, each developer, tester, architect, project manager, principal consultant and so on, just found an extra 21 mins a day (35 hour week) then they would reach 80%. So, great let's do it, its achievable, the data proves it!

Or does it?

Whilst the theory may be right, in reality it's quite likely that each person, depending on their level and the depth of knowledge they have, can only feasibility work on a few matters / cases or projects at any one time?

Because there are only so many items that anyone can practically cope with at any one point. Trying to get your head around something in 20 minutes is pointless as most likely all that will result is one doing re-work the next time, trying to remember what you considered?

We know this to be true from our own experiences, gathering that data and analysing why we couldn't just squeeze in a few more minutes on a new task.

Bottom line, one just can't. Of course one can work longer hours and be incentivised for that, but that's changing the analytical parameters!

The same is true for say a cost saving, efficiency lens. If the data shows that you can get rid of 10.65 people, then that's not going to be possible. You simply can't get rid of 0.65 of a person unless they are only part time.

So the second piece of practical advice is, **it has to work. It has to be deliverable in reality not in theory.**

You will lose hearts and minds if you don't consider things holistically.

Seek and you will find.

Technical operations / effectiveness.

Many IT departments have or are moving towards a continuous integration / deployment model. When this insurer automated their deployments, they found that too often they then had to spend too much time manually fixing the deployment. Which was defeating the object. They were wondering when having followed the same steps consistently, that some deployments were successful, and some weren't.

Tracking when they fail, why they failed, they gathered the data over a 6 month period. Enough of a sample size from the relevant systems, such as their deployment tool, code repository and service desk system. They extracted the data, analysed and created visualisations using Power BI. From this there were able to identify the themes.

We're not saying what they found , but it could easily have involved the age of the application, the level of customisation and bespoke code, the underlying release, patch levels of the data platform, time of deployment, and even the people and skills involved, despite being automated. They could also better predict whether a deployment was going to outright fail, with all the user downtime issues that might entail or whether the deployment simply wasn't perfect, with users largely quite happily continuing working effectively.

From all of this they calculated the impact in terms of user downtime, deployment time and costs and combined with their risk deployment profile could implement a roadmap of solutions to resolve their automated deployment issues.

Be careful what you collect.

In thinking about whatever improvements you wish to make please bear in mind that, as we stated earlier, that you are likely to have certain data protection obligations to whoever the regulator in charge is. In the UK that is currently the Information Commissioners Office (ICO).

Generalising, you should think very carefully about what personal / special data you're holding, thinking of holding, processing and so on.

The ICO advise undertaking a Data Protection Impact Assessment to assess the impact of changes or new solutions. If you are concerned about your current compliance this is also a helpful guide for existing applications too.

Key Message

Be careful what data you try to collect.

Key Message 27 - Be careful what data you collect.

Don't be dull.

We'll keep this simple. If you just do the same old things, you'll get the same old answer won't you?

"Insanity is doing the same thing over and over and expecting different results." (Albert Einstein)

So stop re-inventing the wheel. Stop re-presenting the finance figures as a dashboard. You might have a nice, neat dashboard but the CEO will still just remember you as the dashboard person.

You must make data useful, relevant and consumable by the audience. Don't overload your analysis and recommendations with far too many stats, graphs and diagrams. Just enough to enable the discussion and make progress.

What did Berry do?

As we know Berry had been finding it difficult to engage some of the stakeholders in her force. She decided that she couldn't push water up hill.

Tips 'n Techniques (TNT) 27 - You can't push water uphill.

So she stopped trying, for now. Instead she focused on those areas where there were some willing stakeholders, and working together they could make a difference. In this case she focused on people logistics and scheduling.

Initially these were focused on sporting events / days where there were large numbers of people, all descending on a city centre to watch their favourite team play in international competitions. In summary they combined data from various internal and external sources, including graphical information systems. They predicted which city centre areas were likely to be the optimum places to position their front line officers and constables. Also where their back up or specialist resources could be held in case they were needed. This proved a success.

It is a fairly simple use case these days and has been used across many industries for many years. For example roadside assistance firms, predicting where to place their engineers and vehicles, when looking at holiday travel and weather forecasts. Equipment maintenance service providers, similarly, perhaps adding in where the equipment warranty period was expiring and/or the overall age of equipment was beyond a certain point.

As we noted earlier, if it isn't broken, don't fix it.

Most contact centres will already have a scheduling tool deployed to help with workforce planning. Inevitably these will be considering things like available staff, holidays and predicated call influx and patterns. The same is true for field based resources like the equipment maintenance providers. In other words, this data is already being captured by these specialist applications and no doubt being provided and used by their user schedulers.

So, don't ask these stakeholders what data are you capturing? (To help plan people logistics). Ask:

> Where would the data come from, that you would like to capture, that you think will make a difference to your people logistics?

If that data is already being captured by a different application, then you may have the basis for a potentially useful Power BI use case?

As a simple example. Many organisations have a CRM system to help them manage their customer relationships, be that in a contact centre or throughout the organisation.

As above, the contact centre probably also has a specialist, separate workforce scheduling package.

Let's say that customer complaints, also have their own application solution.

We're not suggesting that it's correct to have, in this case, 3 separate applications nor are we saying that having them all in one application is the right answer. It is likely to be different in each organisation. We're simply saying in our example there are 3 applications.

Hence a question could be:

> Is there accessible data, that when combined and made available to the right people, in the right way, could offer a different view? And hence some better value insight?

We said, "*don't be dull*" and we mean it. However there's a difference between simply re-producing the same stuff that someone else is already doing and finding value in dull places.

This following old British and Irish phrase essentially means, that dirty and unpleasant activities can be lucrative. Herein we're suggesting your inquisitive thinking could be applied to things that don't seem very exciting, they may be boring and tedious, but you can still unearth significant value from that.

Tips 'n Techniques (TNT) 28 - Where there's muck, there's brass!

Berry's example may not the most glamorous. But there is a lot of cost in managing where people should be best deployed.

If people were better deployed, so that they were more likely to be in the right place at the right time to prevent a disturbance or worse, they would be making more effective use of their resources.

They would be dealing with root causes, mitigating and preventing future costs being incurred; not just by the police but by other 3rd parties too in dealing with the aftermath of disturbances.

Furthermore the policemen and women may well feel they were being of use. Which is what many of them joined up for in the first place.

Key Message

Work together, you can make a difference.

Key Message 28 - Work together, make a difference.

However, going back to our examples on utilisation. If say you were in a contact centre and you really wanted to find time to focus on outbound customer retention calls. You probably could make a call in 21 mins? Over the week that's nearly an hour and a half.

Even if you could just retain one more customer using that time.

Would it be worth it?

Or if utilisation was more about space, such as in a warehouse. If you could free up just one more location, shelf, rack.

What would you do with that?

Can Power BI deal with elephant in the room?

There have been two challenges listed on our list of challenges when it comes to building a data driven culture that we haven't listed as Power BI being able to help with, those are:

- ○ Executive support
- ○ Resistance to change.

We sometimes refer to these as the elephant in the room.

Figure 30 - What about the elephant in the room?

You might think that Power BI can't help with these? Granted Power BI can't directly get executive support, nor can it remove resistance to change. Your efforts are vital to these.

What it can do though is support your initiatives in this area.

Executive Support – We've consistently suggested that you start small and demonstrate the value that it brings. There are a number of example application area ideas throughout this book. Maybe some of them apply to you. Here's a couple more.

For example if you are driving this from an IT angle you can use Power BI to show the ROI on your developers by visualising the GIT commits and releases from your CI/CD pipeline so you can show the value that your developers are bringing the organisation. If you are trying to drive this from a business angle you could use your cloud data to show the increase in uptime, or reduction in costs as a result of the changes you have made moving from on premises to cloud technology.

Or let's say you work in marketing, and you want to show the ROI of a particular campaign, or how a campaign led to more sales leads, or what types of promotional activity best suited a customer segment or product type? You can take website traffic data from Google analytics; customer take up interest from CRM and combine with Email Marketing (and other promotion communication tools /methods). You could see in detail not just how the promotion resulted in more leads, which led to more sales. But what were the optimum choices for the future encompassing say channel, promotion type, product type, time of day, type of message, type of call to action etc.

Nothing gets buy in from decision makers like showing how the top and bottom lines will change favourably and help drive the business objectives forward.

Resistance to change - The same would go for resistance to change. "*Seeing is believing*"! If you make it real for the person, they are far more likely to engage. But don't forget, if someone is resisting the change, they are in essence objecting to that change.

And objections are there to be handled. So you must try and handle these.

There is power in numbers. If you're doing the right things, engaging with all stakeholders, gaining agreement, ensuring there is value, getting enough of the right skills and resources deployed, working with the culture you have and towards the one you'd like to reach, handling the concerns as they arise; it is highly likely that you will if not initially, then eventually get buy in.

Comments like "this is the way we've always done things around here" are likely to be in the minority. Even if you do continue to meet some small scale resistance, just remember that for the significant majority you will have delivered something beneficial.

To deliver value, things do not need to be perfect, just good enough. Apply the 80/20 rule.

Key Message

Good enough, is good enough.

Key Message 29 - Good enough is good enough.

Resistance will wain when the benefits become clear.

Change causes worry, worry causes resistance. Remove the worry, remove the problem.

DATA-DRIVEN HAS DELIVERED MANY BENEFITS.

Granted you can list, what we call technology companies, businesses that started with a data driven culture and been successful. We're thinking, Amazon, Netflix, Uber etc. But maybe those organisations are relatively new compared to yours and they don't have the history or longevity compared to say Berry's Police Force.

Here are some examples of what we will call traditional organisations that have needed to change to a data driven culture, not build the data driven culture from the ground up and the success that is has brought them.

Domino's Pizza: Domino's Pizza is an interesting example of a company that has built a data culture in a non-traditional industry. By investing in data collection and analysis tools, Domino's has been able to gain insights into customer preferences and behaviour. This has helped the company make data-driven decisions about everything from menu offerings to delivery routes, leading to increased customer satisfaction and improved business outcomes.

Walmart: Walmart is one of the world's largest retailers, and it has built a strong data culture to support its operations. By collecting data on customer purchases and supply chain logistics, Walmart is able to optimize its inventory management and pricing strategies. The company has also invested in data analytics tools to help it better understand customer behaviour and preferences, which has led to improved customer satisfaction and increased sales.

Procter & Gamble: Procter & Gamble is a consumer goods company that has embraced data analytics to help it stay ahead of its competitors. By collecting data on customer feedback and market trends, Procter & Gamble is able to make data-driven decisions about product development and marketing strategies. The company has also invested in data visualisation tools to help employees better understand and interpret the data they collect, leading to more informed decision-making.

Ford: Ford is an automotive company that has been using data analytics to improve its operations for many years. By collecting data on everything from supply chain logistics to customer preferences, Ford is able to optimize its manufacturing processes and develop products that better meet customer needs. The company has also invested in data-driven marketing campaigns, which has helped it increase sales and improve customer loyalty.

If you are reading this and thinking, these are all profit making private companies, these don't apply to me, I work in the public sector and things work differently there. Here are some of examples of data culture being fostered in the UK public sector:

NHS Digital: NHS Digital is responsible for providing digital and data services to the National Health Service (NHS) in England. The organisation has invested in data infrastructure and analytics tools to support its operations, and it has developed a culture that values the collection and analysis of data. NHS Digital collects and analyse s data on everything from patient health outcomes to hospital admissions, and it uses this data to inform its policies and programs. By building a data culture, NHS Digital has been able to improve the quality of healthcare services provided to patients across England.

Office for National Statistics (ONS): The ONS is the UK's official statistics agency, and it has embraced a data-driven approach to policy development and decision-making. The agency collects data on everything from population demographics to economic indicators, and it uses this data to inform its statistical outputs and reports. The ONS has invested in data analytics tools and visualisation software to help employees better understand and interpret the data they collect. By building a data culture, the ONS has been able to provide accurate and timely statistics that support evidence-based decision-making in the UK.

HM Revenue and Customs (HMRC): HMRC is responsible for collecting taxes and enforcing tax laws in the UK. The organisation has invested in data infrastructure and analytics tools to support its operations, and it has developed a culture that values the collection and analysis of data. HMRC collects and analyse s data on everything from tax compliance to economic trends, and it uses this data to inform its policies and programs. By building a data culture, HMRC has been able to identify areas where tax compliance can be improved and has been successful in reducing the tax gap between what is owed and what is collected.

SUMMARY

We thought we'd start our summary by asking.

Does anybody actually want a data driven culture?

Well they might say they do, and if so, happy days! However we believe what they really mean is,

They want the benefits it brings.

Which is great. Because that brings us right back to our top key message.

Start with why.

Assume nothing. Find out. Do some investigation, some analysis, some what if scenarios. For example, if your leaders say they want a data driven culture, and you ask them if they mean that they want the benefits it brings. (They will say yes). Then you can not only ask them what the benefits are they are seeking; you can try and uncover how they think becoming more data driven might bring these benefits.

In so doing you'll be walking the walk, gaining some buy-in and building some evidence of how things could change. You'll be building your vision, your support and starting to develop your business case. Keep the big picture in mind and align it to the business strategy and objectives.

Showing how the new data driven culture will deliver the mission of the business will help you get that key buy-in from key stakeholders that you will need to make your change successful.

Remember this is unlikely to be a change that can delivered overnight in a big bang approach. You will need to start small and increase the data maturity of your organisation in small increments. Start with the low hanging fruit and remember to take people with you on the journey. You can't achieve your goal without them.

Don't talk about data!

Use language that people understand.

Talk about their roles, listen to what people do, e.g. Customer service agents, Support officers, Salespeople, Marketing staff, IT operations support, Paralegals, Solicitors, Nurses, Warehouse operatives, Maintenance engineers, Human resource officers and so on. Chat about what they would like to be able to do in their language.

By chatting, we mean go out there and engage. Speak with stakeholders, ask them questions, listen, check you understand, find out how much of a difference changing things would really mean.

Do you remember,

> The six honest serving men?
>
> The 5 whys?
>
> The VIPP framework?
>
> Keep your project on a page?

These are all, in our opinion, great techniques to use to engage people.

What are you going to do from here?

Overall, building a data culture in an organisation requires a commitment to change and a willingness to invest in the necessary resources and infrastructure to support the use of data. With the right approach, organisations can build a data-driven culture that helps them make better decisions and achieve their goals.

So what approach are you going to take?

You could:

> Use Plan - Do - Check - Act? Maybe you feel you've done plan and do, so perhaps go back, read the contents page and check out what you want to revisit. Then act on that.
>
> Or you could go forward and read our summary lists? We've complied lists of LOAP's, Key messages, TNT's, Quotes, References, and Figures we've used. Perhaps some of these are the things to bear in mind as you progress?

Whatever you do; crack on and hold some workshops, seek out some advice or training, buy in some expertise, make sure you're comfortable that you have, learn or find the know-how to do it. Reach out if you think we can help you.

Final things to say.

We wanted to leave you with one more TNT and Key message.

You might have noticed that we keep repeating things. That's because it's well proven, common sense method to embed learning. It may well be a familiar technique but it's not just to confirm getting your point across. You can also use the principle to check that you understand, test your deliverables and confirm the outcomes are met.

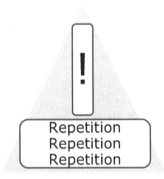

Tips 'n Techniques (TNT) 29 - Repetition, Repetition, Repetition.

You might have also noticed that we keep repeating, coming back to the people. That's because, at the end of the day, it's the people that do it, they make things happen.

Key Message

People make it happen.

Key Message 30 - People make it happen.

And as a final quote, remember as a wise man once said,

"If you really don't worry too much about who gets the credit, delivering change can be easier than it sometimes appears." (Wise Man!)

Good luck with your data journey.

A LIST OF THINGS WE'VE USED.

Here's a list of the:

Learning on a Page (LOAP's)

Key messages

Tips 'n techniques (TNT)

Quotes

References and

Figures

that we have used within this book. Use it however it helps you.

Learning on a page (LOAP) - A List

LOAP - Learning on a Page 1 - Key Change Considerations.

LOAP - Learning on a Page 2 - First things to know.

LOAP - Learning on a Page 3 - First things to remember.

LOAP - Learning on a Page 4 - How to start.

LOAP - Learning on a Page 5 - How to establish leadership support.

LOAP - Learning on a Page 6 - How to build a data driven mindset.

LOAP - Learning on a Page 7 - Strategies for overcoming resistance to change.

LOAP - Learning on a Page 8 - A step by step guide to building a data driven culture.

Key messages

Key Message 1 - Do you really know-how to do it?

Key Message 2 - People, Process, Data, Technology.

Key Message 3 - Actions speak louder than words.

Key Message 4 - Data always exists!

Key Message 5 - Data culture aligns to organisational culture.

Key Message 6 - Know why.

Key Message 7 - You must pass the so what test.

Key Message 8 - Do the right things.

Key Message 9 - Change, of any sort, is not easy.

Key Message 10 - Too many projects fail. Often down to people and resources.

Key Message 11 - Know how to decide before you decide.

Key Message 12 - Break things down into bite sized pieces.

Key Message 13 - Culture is top down and bottom up.

Key Message 14 - You can't build on shifting sand.

Key Message 15 - LUCK is Labour under correct knowledge.

Key Message 16 - Under promise, over deliver.

Key Message 17 - Seeing is believing.

Key Message 18 - You need to win hearts and minds.

Key Message 19 - A lack of vision leads to confusion.

Key Message 20 - A lack of agreement leads to sabotage.

Key Message 21 - Skin in the game is vital.

Key Message 22 - A picture paints ten thousand words.

Key Message 23 - Practice what you preach. Key

Message 24 - Start with the end in mind.

Key Message 25 - Right Data Story, Right People, Right Place, Right Time.

Key Message 26 - Beware of Lies, Dammed Lies and Statistics.

Key Message 27 - Be careful what data you collect.

Key Message 28 - Work together, make a difference.

Key Message 29 - Good enough is good enough.

Key Message 30 - People make it happen.

Tips 'n techniques (TNT)

Tips 'n Techniques (TNT) 1 - Do not assume.

Tips 'n Techniques (TNT) 2 - Culture eats strategy for breakfast.

Tips 'n Techniques (TNT) 3 - Clarity does not mean certainty.

Tips 'n Techniques (TNT) 4 - If it isn't broken don't fix it.

Tips 'n Techniques (TNT) 5 - Projects fail because of people.

Tips 'n Techniques (TNT) 6 - Projects fail because of funding.

Tips 'n Techniques (TNT) 7 - Fit your approach to your culture.

Tips 'n Techniques (TNT) 8 - Failing to plan, is planning to fail.

Tips 'n Techniques (TNT) 9 - Measure twice, cut once.

Tips 'n Techniques (TNT) 10 - When you assume, you make an ass out of you and me.

Tips 'n Techniques (TNT) 11 - Timing is everything.

Tips 'n Techniques (TNT) 12 - Garbage in, garbage out.

Tips 'n Techniques (TNT) 13 - Start small.

Tips 'n Techniques (TNT) 14 - More haste, less speed.

Tips 'n Techniques (TNT) 15 - Ask what if?

Tips 'n Techniques (TNT) 16 - Know your audience.

Tips 'n Techniques (TNT) 17 - Vision is everything.

Tips 'n Techniques (TNT) 18 - Change is a marathon, not a sprint.

Tips 'n Techniques (TNT) 19 - You need vision, agreement, sponsorship.

Tips 'n Techniques (TNT) 20 - You never get a second chance to make a first impression.

Tips 'n Techniques (TNT) 21 - Ask the same question in different ways.

Tips 'n Techniques (TNT) 22 - Find the golden thread.

Tips 'n Techniques (TNT) 23 - Develop your business case.

Tips 'n Techniques (TNT) 24 - Objections are buying signals.

Tips 'n Techniques (TNT) 25 - What's in it for me?

Tips 'n Techniques (TNT) 26 - www.com

Tips 'n Techniques (TNT) 27 - You can't push water uphill.

Tips 'n Techniques (TNT) 28 - Where there's muck, there's brass!

Tips 'n Techniques (TNT) 29 - Repetition, Repetition, Repetition.

Quotes

"The ROI for companies that invest in coaching is 7 Times the initial investment" (PWC 2011).

"To know thyself is the beginning of wisdom." (Socrates)

"All Models are flawed although some are useful." (George Box)

"The only constant in life is change." (Heraclitus)

Paraphrasing (CS Lewis) *"Things are rarely, ever the same twice."*

"So you're saying, common sense seems to be, not all that common!" (A trusted friend)

"Customer expectations? Nonsense. No customer ever asked for the electric light, the pneumatic tire, the VCR, or the CD. All customer expectations are only what you and your competitor have led him to expect. He knows nothing else." (W Edwards Deming)

"In any moment of decision, the best thing you can do is the right thing, the next best thing is the wrong thing, and the worst thing you can do is nothing." (Theodore Roosevelt)

"It is not necessary to change. Survival is not mandatory.". (W Edwards Deming)

"If you can't fit it on an envelope, it's rubbish!" (Richard Branson)

"Organisation culture refers to the shared values, beliefs, behaviours, customs, and practices that shape the behaviour of individuals within an organisation. Organisational culture is the collective personality of the organisation and how it influences how people interact with each other, how decisions are made, and how work is done." (Our summary of various sources such as, Ravasi and Schultz, Dean and Kennedy, Kotter)

"Change will not come if we wait for some other person or some other time. We are the ones we've been waiting for. We are the change that we seek." (Barack Obama)

"Clarity doesn't mean certainty". (Us)

"We have two ears and one mouth, for a reason, to listen first!" (Anonymous)

"Seek to understand before you seek to be understood." (Stephen Covey)

"I keep six honest serving men (they taught me all I knew); Their names are What and Why and When and How and Where and Who." (Rudyard Kipling)

"Begin each day with a clear vision of your desired direction and destination, and then continue flexing your proactive muscles to make things happen." (Stephen Covey)

"People don't resist change; they resist being changed." (Peter Senge)

"Start at the beginning, it's a very good place to start." (Julie Andrews / Rogers & Hammerstein!)

"A happy customer tells a friend; an unhappy customer tells the world." (Unknown)

"Nothing great was ever achieved without enthusiasm." (Ralph Waldo Emerson)

"Without ambition one starts nothing Without work one finishes nothing. The prize will not be sent to you. You have to win it." (Ralph Waldo Emerson)

"Life is a journey, not a destination." (Ralph Waldo Emerson)

"No plan survives conflict with the enemy." (Army General)

"The most important advice I give to young people is … just learn how to get stuff done." (Barack Obama)

Taking a liberty with this great quote. *"It doesn't make sense to hire smart people and then ~~tell them what to do~~ ignore them; we hire smart people so they can tell us what to do."* – (Steve Jobs)

"I think it's almost impossible for a smart person to win in business in America today, because I find smart people spend their whole lifetime figuring things out. They always trying to figure out an easier way, and a quicker way. And another thing I found out about smart people; is they just don't get around to doing nothing." (Art Williams)

"It doesn't make sense to hire smart people and then tell them what to do; we hire smart people so they can tell us what to do." (Steve Jobs)

"There are three kinds of lies: Lies, damned lies, and statistics." (Mark Twain. Others attribute it to British Prime Minister Benjamin Disraeli.) Maybe neither said it.

"Insanity is doing the same thing over and over and expecting different results." (Albert Einstein)

"If you really don't worry too much about who gets the credit, delivering change can be easier than it sometimes appears." (Wise Man!)

References and resources

These were correct and relevant links accessed as of 16/08/2023.

Art Williams, *"Just Do It!"* This was a speech originally delivered by Art Williams at the 1987 National Religious Broadcaster Convention. If you wish to see the speech, it's not long and well worth it, it's here: https://youtu.be/TU7Y6HiLXto

Start with Why by Simon Sinek. Our e-book copy indicates: First published in the USA by Portfolio Penguin, a member of Penguin Group (USA) Inc. 2009. First published in the Great Britain by Portfolio Penguin 2011. Published in Penguin Business 2019. You can also find out more about Simon's business here www.startwithwhy.com

Pulse of the Profession - The Project Management Institute (PMI) (2017) https://www.pmi.org/-/media/pmi/documents/public/pdf/learning/thought-leadership/pulse/pulse-of-the-profession-2017.pdf

Frank Faeth in 2022, updated *IT Project Failure Rates: Facts and Reasons* having been written several. Includes following statistics:

- *According to the Standish Group's Annual CHAOS 2020 report, 66% of technology projects (based on the analysis of 50,000 projects globally) end in partial or total failure.*

- *Research from McKinsey in 2020 found that 17% of large IT projects go so badly, they threaten the very existence of the company!*

- *BCG (2020) estimated that 70% of digital transformation efforts fall short of meeting targets.*

You can also find out more about Frank's business here: *https://faethcoaching.com/it-project-failure-rates-facts-and-reasons/#:~:text=they%20were%20challenged.-,%27,fall%20short%20of%20meeting%20targets*

"Organisation culture refers to the shared values, beliefs, behaviours, customs, and practices that shape the behaviour of individuals within an organisation. Organisational culture is the collective personality of the organisation and how it influences how people interact with each other, how decisions are made, and how work is done". (Our summary of various sources such as, Ravasi and Schultz (2006), Dean and Kennedy (1982), Kotter)

> Ravasi and Schultz (2006) *Responding to organisational identity threats: Exploring the role of organizational culture" Academy of Management Journal 49 (3) 433-458.* We found that on Wikipedia.
>
> Dean and Kennedy (1982) Theory of Organizational Culture. *Corporate Cultures: The Rites and Rituals of Corporate Life.*
>
> Kotter. You can also find out more about Dr John Kotter's business here https://www.kotterinc.com/services/culture-change/

Gartner 2017 Annual Chief Data Officer https://www.gartner.com/en/newsroom/press-releases/2017-12-06-gartner-survey-finds-chief-data-officers-are-delivering-business-impact-and-enabling-digital-transformation

"Managing Successful Programmes" (MSP) 2011 Edition. Published by TSO (The Stationery Office) www.tsoshop.co.uk

The Lippitt-Knoster model for managing complex change. We believe the original source was Mary Lippitt (The Managing Complex Change Model) from 1987, although Timothy Knoster is understood to have used it in a TASH conference in 1991.

Prosci's *Best Practices in Change Management*. *https://www.prosci.com/resources/articles/change-management-best-practices*

Figures

Figure 1 - Know-how definitions.

Figure 2 - Organisational culture definitions.

Figure 3 - Common drivers for change.

Figure 4 - Must change only be objective?

Figure 5 - Assessing your know-how 1.

Figure 6 - Assessing your know-how 2.

Figure 7 - Example RACI guide.

Figure 8 - Steps involved in changing data culture.

Figure 9 - Plan - Do - Check - Act.

Figure 10 - Specific data culture challenges facing CDO's.

Figure 11 - Definition of Data Literacy.

Figure 12 - Our VIPP framework.

Figure 13 - Data Dimension examples.

Acknowledgements

As we stated at the start of this book. Over the years we have both seen an awful lot of Change, from small to truly transformational. Our reputations are built on practical, common sense approaches, getting the job done and delivering the outcomes.

We have worked with many, many people over the years and we would like to thank all of you, whether you were customers, colleagues, suppliers, coaches, mentors or contacts. You've been a pleasure to work with and many thanks for all that you helped us to learn.

We would also like to thank our families and friends for putting up with us and freely providing your help in the writing, critique, editing, proof reading and publication of this book.

And to our readers, once again:

We hope you find something of value herein, that you can easily put into use.

If in doubt, be positive!

Start somewhere, make a difference.

What would make a difference to us is if you were willing to provide us some feedback, a rating or a review. Thanks.

Printed in Poland
by Amazon Fulfillment
Poland Sp. z o.o., Wrocław

36522998R00141